THE LONGITUDE PRIZE

THE
LONGITUDE PRIZE

Joan Dash

Pictures by Dušan Petričić

Frances Foster Books

Farrar, Straus and Giroux ∽ New York

Library of Congress Cataloging-in-Publication Data
Dash, Joan.
    The longitude prize / Joan Dash, Dušan Petričić, illus. — 1st ed.
        p.   cm.
    "Frances Foster books."
    Summary: The story of John Harrison, inventor of watches and clocks, who spent forty
years working on a time-machine which could be used to accurately determine longitude
at sea.
    ISBN 0-374-34636-4
    1. Chronometers—History—Juvenile literature. 2. Longitude—Measurement—
History—Juvenile literature. 3. Harrison, John, 1693–1776—Juvenile literature.
4. Clocks and watch makers—Great Britain—Biography—Juvenile literature.
[1. Harrison, John, 1693–1776. 2. Clocks and watches. 3. Inventors.] I. Title.

QB107.D28   2000
681.1′1′092—dc21
[B]
                                                                          97-044257

To the Bottman brothers,
Sam and Nate,
with whom the author has shared many remarkable adventures

Grateful thanks for advice and kind encouragement to
Dr. Fred Brown, Emeritus Professor, Physics, University of Washington;
Dr. Greg Dash, Emeritus Professor, Physics, University of Washington;
Paul Middents, Adjunct Professor, Astronomy and Mathematics,
Olympic College, Bremerton.

CONTENTS

THE LONGITUDE PRIZE

1

·

"A MOST TERRIBLE SEA"

At six in the morning I was awaked
by a great shock, and a confused noise
of the men on deck. I ran up, thinking some
ship had run foul of us, for by my own reckoning, and that of
every other person in the ship, we were at least thirty-five leagues
distant from land; but, before I could reach the quarter-deck,
the ship gave a great stroke upon the ground, and the sea broke
over her. Just after this I could perceive the land, rocky, rugged
and uneven, about two cables' length from us . . . the masts soon

went overboard, carrying some men with them . . . notwith-standing a most terrible sea, one of the [lifeboats] was launched, and eight of the best men jumped into her; but she had scarcely got to the ship's stern when she was hurled to the bottom, and every soul in her perished. The rest of the boats were soon washed to pieces on the deck. We then made a raft . . . and waited with resignation for Providence to assist us.

—From an account of the wreck of HMS
Litchfield off the coast of North Africa, 1758

The *Litchfield* came to grief because no one aboard knew where they were. As the narrator tells us, by his own reckoning and that of everyone else they were supposed to be thirty-five leagues, about a hundred miles, from land. The word "reckoning" was short for "dead reckoning"—the system used by ships at sea to keep track of their position, meaning their longitude and latitude. It was an intricate system, a craft, and like every other craft involved the mastery of certain tools, in this case such instruments as compass, hourglass, and quadrant. It was an art as well.

Latitude, the north–south position, had always been the navigator's faithful guide. Even in ancient times, a Greek or Roman sailor could tell how far north of the equator he was by observing the North Star's height above the horizon, or the sun's at noon. This could be done without instruments, trusting in experience and the naked eye, although it is believed that an ancestor of the quadrant called the astrolabe—"star-measurer"—was known to the ancients, and used by them to measure the angular height of the sun or a star above the horizon.

Phoenicians, Greeks, and Romans tended to sail along the coasts and were rarely out of sight of land. As later navigators left the safety of the Mediterranean to plunge into the vast Atlantic—far from shore, and from the shorebirds that led them to it—they still had the sun and the North Star. And these enabled them to follow imagined parallel lines of latitude that circle the globe. Following a line of latitude—"sailing the parallel"—kept a ship on a steady east–west course. Christopher Columbus, who sailed the parallel in 1492, held his ships on such a safe course, west and west again, straight on toward Asia. When they came across an island off the coast of what would later be called America, Columbus compelled his crew to sign an affidavit stating that this island was no island but mainland Asia.

A hundred years later, in Shakespeare's *The Merchant of Venice*, one of his characters discusses trade with Mexico and the West Indies as a risky but established business. For the great voyages of exploration that followed Columbus were followed in turn by an explosion of international commerce. There was intense competition for goods and markets. Naval and merchant vessels jammed the familiar sea-lanes, the safe courses, where pirates lay in wait for them. Piracy, too, had become a flourishing trade.

And all of them, whether pirate, merchant, or naval vessel, had to crowd into the familiar sea-lanes based on latitude—because longitude, the east–west location, was not straightforward or reliable. Longitude was an awesome, mysterious, perhaps unknowable secret. It was the seaman's pot of gold, his will-o'-the wisp, his misfortune, his curse, sometimes his deadly enemy.

This is how a navigator in the era of Columbus kept track of longitude. Having set his direction in a rough and ready way with the compass, he would throw a chunk of wood overboard from the bows. Suppose his 50-foot ship took 10 seconds—timed with the hourglass—to pass the wooden chunk, and his compass told him he was sailing west. He was making 300 feet a minute, then, about 3½ miles an hour. The number of miles made in the course of the day were then added to those recorded in his books. He knew how long ago they had left Madeira—a usual departure point because it lay in the latitude of the trade winds—and he had a general idea of Madeira's longitude. After making allowance for the winds and the current, he would try to reckon how far west of Madeira he had sailed. He might be right. More often he would be wrong by sixty, eighty, or many hundreds of miles.

A coastline our navigator believed to lie three hundred miles west of him might suddenly loom up out of the mist, too close for anything but disaster. It was no less likely that the longed-for coast—promising food, water, shelter—dodged and escaped him because he had already left it far behind. A vessel blown off course by storms might sail about aimlessly for weeks, searching for land first eastward, then westward, while the food supply dwindled, and men began dying from thirst, hunger, and scurvy. Soon so few were left they could no longer handle the rigging, and they drifted, as one by one the last survivors died; then even the rats died. The ship had become a ghost ship peopled by skeletons. By the start of the eighteenth century, untold thousands of sailors had perished because they had no way of knowing their longitude.

Several of the great naval powers—Spain, Portugal, Venice, France—offered princely rewards, or lifetime pensions, for any sure solution to the mystery of longitude at sea. In 1675, the Royal Observatory at Greenwich, England, was built for that purpose, "to find out the so much desired Longitude at Sea, for the perfecting the art of Navigation." But the British did not offer a reward; not yet.

A tragedy at sea was partly responsible for the government's change of heart. Twenty-one ships of the Royal Navy were sailing homeward from Gibraltar in 1707, each ship with its own navigator, the whole fleet under the command of an admiral with the curious name of Sir Clowdisley Shovell.

The weather was nasty: there were gales, squalls, and heavily overcast skies. After three weeks the skies brightened and several ships got observations of latitude; soundings were taken for depth. When Sir Clowdisley called his navigators together, all agreed they were on the edge of the Continental Shelf, approaching the entrance to the English Channel.

The skies clouded up again, and the fleet sailed on, running eastward before a favorable gale. On October 22, at about seven-thirty in the evening, four of the ships rammed into a reef off the Scilly Isles, some twenty miles west of Cornwall. Within the space of a few hours all four injured ships went down, along with the men they carried. Some accounts claim there were eight hundred dead; some put the number at two thousand. There had been other shipwrecks recently, there would be many more to come, but the scale of the loss this time—four battleships, and those hundreds of sailors, murdered without an enemy in sight—made a powerful impression on the British mind.

Everyone thought the tragedy was due to ignorance of the ships' position, but in recent years historians have begun to see the shipwreck off the Scilly Isles in a different light. It is believed that when the admiral consulted with his navigators, their findings were correct—that they knew where they were, and where they wanted to go, and that the disaster was caused by the maps and charts they used.

Accurate charts for a sailing ship must be made from aboard ship, and with accurate knowledge of longitude, for the longitude serves two purposes. It provides the navigator with reliable maps and charts. And once he's at sea, it tells him where he is, enabling him to use those charts.

English ships had been sailing everywhere in the Western world, relying on charts and maps that often had little relation to reality.

Even at home, there were coastlines whose charts might have been purposely created to lead ships to their death. The Scilly Isles were just such a place, lawless and primitive, their rocky shores unlit and unmarked. The inhabitants were said to live by plundering shipwrecks, which might have explained the absence of lights or channel markers—they were indeed luring ships to their death.

Whatever the direct cause of the disaster—inaccurate maps, or faulty navigation—the root cause was ignorance of the longitude. The public outcry that followed led to an act of Parliament, in 1714, offering a prize that was greater than those of other countries, since Britain had the world's largest and most important merchant fleet. Any device or invention for determining longitude that "shall have been Tried and found Practicable and useful at Sea" would be rewarded with 20,000 pounds.

It was an enormous sum, roughly equal to $12 million today, and lesser awards were offered for partial solutions. The nation's leading scientists, Sir Isaac Newton and Edmond Halley among them, pursued the prize, as did the wildest crackpots, yet even fifty years later it was still untouched.

News of the longitude prize reached America, and came to the attention of a young man named Thomas Godfrey. He was a glazier, his work was the fitting and installing of glass panes, but his great love was mathematics. John Hadley, an English gentleman-farmer interested in optics, also learned about the prize. Some fifteen years after it was first announced, each of them, knowing nothing about the other, informed authorities in England of an instrument he had invented that might one day help solve the longitude problem. As it happened, as so often happens in the history of science, they had invented the same instrument more or less simultaneously.

News of the prize made its way to Barrow-upon-Humber, nearly two hundred miles from London, in an isolated part of Lincolnshire. John Harrison, the village carpenter, heard it and was fired with ambition. Clocks were his passion, all his spare time went into the designing and making of clocks, and he began to think about a seagoing clock that could be used as a longitude device. He planned it out painstakingly on paper.

When he was finally ready to be tested by the world beyond Barrow, he headed for London to present his idea to the Board of Longitude. This Board came into being with the Longitude Act of 1714 and was charged with evaluating any solution submitted to it. Harrison arrived at roughly the same time Godfrey and Hadley were finishing their inventions. It was the start of a race, although none of the three knew they were participating in one. Such was the peculiar nature of this race that Godfrey and Hadley became the first part of a relay team, whose members eventually included some of the noteworthy men of the time. But Harrison ran alone, for he was essentially a loner, plain-spoken, often tactless, with a temper he couldn't always control, and a genius for mechanics.

He was born in the Yorkshire town of Foulby in 1693, the first of five children of Henry Harrison, a carpenter, and his wife, Elizabeth. When the boy was six or seven, the family pulled up stakes and moved sixty miles away to Barrow, a sleepy farming village where nothing much ever happened, and where life had hardly changed since Shakespeare's day. Near the broad Humber River estuary, with the North Sea breathing coldly on it from the east, Barrow was little more than a straggle of cottages, a church, an inn, with farmland all around, flat, featureless, and marshy.

Little is known about John Harrison's early years, for the Harrisons were humble people, and the doings of such people seldom leave any traces behind. There are no letters, no diaries, no memoirs; everyone was too busy with the demands of daily life to do any writing about it. The result is that more than his early life escapes us—the man himself is hard to get at.

Other actors in this story leave paper trails, from which something can be learned about the inner self. But Harrison has to be pieced together with odds and ends plucked from pamphlets he published later on, or from his writings about his work. Dedicated admirers have done exactly that: stitched his character as well as they could out of bits and pieces. There are periods of his life when we see him somewhat more clearly, but his childhood is not one of them.

We know that his father, Henry Harrison, served as parish clerk, which tells us he could read and write; in addition to carpentry, the father did some land surveying, so he would have had to know arithmetic, algebra, and geometry as well. Maybe he had attended a village school in Foulby. Much of England was illiterate at the time, and it's unlikely that a place as remote as Barrow had any sort of school, so whatever book learning the Harrison children had they got at home, from their father. Beyond that level they would have been pretty much on their own, free to find books any way they could, and in the absence of books, to learn from nature, from observation and simple experiments, or not to learn at all.

In any case, childhood was brief in those days. To keep a growing family fed, clothed, and even moderately warm in winter, every available pair of hands would be needed. A youngster strong enough to use a broom, or carry an armful of firewood, was set to work, usually by the age of twelve. When it was John's turn, he became his father's apprentice in the carpentry shop.

There is no record that he did so, but all the same it's clear that he served such an apprenticeship. His early clocks were made mostly of wood; since he lived in Barrow until adulthood, he must have learned carpentry and the uses of wood where he learned everything else: at home, from his father. It's also clear that within a few years—probably by the time he was eighteen—he longed to learn something more, something beyond the mysteries of wood, although he had a great affection for it. Science was what he wanted to learn; in the eighteenth century it was called natural philosophy.

We know about this from local records unearthed by two Harrison "detectives," Humphrey Quill and William Laycock. Putting both accounts together, the following emerges: in the seventeenth century, a member of the landed gentry in that neighborhood had placed a sum of money in trust so that informal talks could be given once a week in Barrow church by visiting clergymen. These talks were probably religious in nature. Yet there was nothing to prevent some learned minister from pointing out the Almighty's designs— the glories of the heavens, the laws that govern the behavior of earthly matter. John Harrison attended at least one such talk. The minister who delivered it—there is no record of his name—was very much impressed by the young carpenter with a hunger for learning. On a later visit he brought a manuscript copy of some lectures given by Nicholas Saunderson, a remarkable man who had been blind since early childhood, and who became a distinguished Cambridge professor of mathematics and physics.

John was allowed to keep the Saunderson manuscript long enough to make a copy of his own, the many diagrams as well as the text all written out in a neat, scholarly hand. The subjects included optics, the physics of light; hydrostatics, the physics of water pressure; and the free movements of heavenly bodies. They would have presented a serious challenge even to a youngster with solid secondary-school preparation.

John Harrison made notes in the margins of his manuscript copy, scores of them in handwriting that changed over the course of years, showing that he referred to it again and again. This copy was sold in 1921 and has since vanished, but the description of it in the sale catalogue survives. Perhaps the visiting clergyman gave him occasional private lessons. He had no other advanced education.

Yet by the time he was twenty he had learned to make clocks—expertly. In 1713 he completed a pendulum clock, parts of which still exist, and within the next four years he made two more that also survive in parts. How he learned to do it is hard to imagine. The usual way to master a craft as intricate as clockmaking was to go to London and apprentice to an expert there. John Harrison never did this; apprenticeships had to be paid for, and he might not have had the money. It's also possible that London seemed distant and even frightening to a country boy.

We know there was nobody in or near Barrow capable of teaching him, since there is no record of any clockmaker in northern Lincolnshire during that period. So he must have taught himself, in the only possible way: by somehow getting hold of a clock—although they were hard to come by as well as extremely expensive—then taking apart this rare and costly clock, putting it back together, and taking it apart again, over and over until he understood how it worked and could build one of his own. It was an impressive feat, and would be followed by others far more impressive once he took up serious clockmaking.

Those first Harrison clocks were not much different in design from others of the time, except for the nearly universal use of wood. The inner works were mostly oak and boxwood, a very few parts being brass or steel. The wheels were oak, their teeth being separately

carved out of oak, three or four at a time, then fitted into grooves in the rims of the wheels. These clocks were the work of someone who was familiar with wood, who loved and trusted it and knew its secrets.

Although he was first and foremost a carpenter at this stage of his life, his clocks must have earned something of a local reputation, for in his late twenties he was given an important commission. It was Humphrey Quill, Harrison's first biographer, who found the clues by tracking down a descendant of John Harrison's brother.

In 1720 Sir Charles Pelham, the owner of a 30,000-acre estate called Brocklesby Park, some nine miles from Barrow, wanted a tower clock built above his new stables. He sent for Harrison, who had never made such a clock, but would certainly have known the problems. One was the weather: the metal parts of an outdoor clock were bound to rust, and the lubricating oils—goose grease was the most popular—would congeal in winter and thin out in summer, slowing or speeding up the works. In fact, oil was an enemy of accuracy in clocks whether indoors or out. It turned rancid with time and corroded anything it touched. It attracted dust, and as the oil evaporated, an abrasive mixture was formed that cut through metal parts. Only the most sophisticated clockmakers understood any of this at the time.

Harrison the carpenter, who did understand, built the tower clock with bearings of lignum vitae, a dense, heavy tropical hardwood that gives off its own grease. With lignum vitae there could be no buildup of oil, no need for oiling anywhere in the works.

For parts that had to be made of metal, normally iron or steel, he used brass, which could not rust. The wheels were oak; the wooden cabinet enclosing the clock was put together exactly like a piece of fine furniture, using pegged joints, and with the edges of the doors carefully matched to the edges of the case. Everything was close-fitting, partly for protection against pigeons, who might otherwise roost around the clockworks, even nest there. The clock in Brocklesby Park is still in use, still running, and without need for lubrication, although it was finished as long ago as 1722.

By that time John Harrison had begun working with his younger brother James, and what they were working at was serious clockmaking. Apparently they meant to find out what prevented the clocks of their day from keeping absolutely accurate time. Maybe this was part of a business venture, either clock repair or the manufacture of clocks. Maybe it started as a hobby that grew, snowballed, took over their lives. However it happened, John Harrison had embarked on a single-minded quest for perfection. The several clocks that survive from that period, as well as a manuscript written in 1730, are witnesses to the quest.

Although his brother James could and did help, the creative mind was always John's, and we know this from the course their later lives took. James eventually lost interest in clocks. For John, they were always what mattered most in life, so that he brought to the making of his clocks not only a powerful creative imagination but patience—never-ending, seemingly inexhaustible.

He was not patient when it came to people, however. He had a quick, sometimes uncontrollable temper. He had certain fixed ideas that he stuck to. He was hard on himself and hard on others, and was happiest when working—with mechanisms, with equations. Yet he was not unsociable, at least in his youth. We know he took an active role in village life, thanks to local records that show he served as a juror and a constable. He loved music, especially church music; he played the viol, trained the choir, and tuned the bells at Barrow church. He courted a girl and married her, and when she died he courted and married another with the same first name, Elizabeth.

In later life, people often remarked on how modest he was, so it's worth noting that the clocks the brothers produced together were signed only by James, in bold script right across the painted wooden faces. Yet the clock design was done by John, with James acting solely as craftsman. If John was hard-driving, he could be generous as well.

By the time he reached his early thirties, with the help of his younger brother he had created two pendulum clocks that were unlike any others anywhere in Europe.

⸱⟨∞⟩⸱

The first mechanical clocks were tower clocks that came into being during the Middle Ages. Less accurate at first than sundials, their great advantage was that they were large enough and high enough for everyone in the village to see the time at a glance. They were powered by gravity. A cord or chain was wrapped around a drum, with a weight attached to the end of it; as the weight fell, it pulled the line and turned the drum.

The turning drum drove the hands of the clock by means of a series of gears—which also drove a device called an escapement. Every mechanical timekeeper has its escapement, consisting of a small, toothed wheel, the escape wheel, and a curved metal device called a pallet, which engages the teeth of the wheel. As the pallet rocks back and forth, it releases the escape wheel momentarily, allowing it to make a small advance. Then the next tooth is caught and released, then the next after that. The job of the escapement, in other words, is to ration out power, in this case the power of gravity.

Spring-driven clocks developed in the late fifteenth century, and their power came from a coiled spring, the mainspring, that became wound when the clock was wound; the mainspring then slowly unwound, again under the control of the escapement. The use of a spring-driven mechanism led to portable clocks and watches.

The performance of all those early timekeepers, whether large or small, tended to be erratic. It was only in the mid-1600s, with the invention of the pendulum clock, and the hairspring-controlled balance wheel, that it became possible to speak of an accurate clock. The back-and-forth swings of the pendulum are so regular, so dependable, that each turn of the escape wheel, each of its rockings that catch and then release the pallet, come under reliable control.

By the early years of the eighteenth century, clocks of astonishing accuracy were being produced. They lost or gained no more than several seconds a week. It was that smattering of seconds that stood between the very best clocks and something approaching perfection.

The wonderful clocks that John Harrison built with his brother's help were made mostly of wood, like the early clocks he had made himself. They had the brass escape wheel, also like the early ones. But almost everything else had been rethought and redesigned. Perhaps the brothers had already heard about the great prize; John might have stored it away in some corner of his mind as a distant, unlikely, but splendid goal that lay at the end of a very long road. They were still carpenters, after all, so their clockmaking had to be done in whatever time they could spare from earning a living.

This is how John Harrison rethought the pendulum. It was well known at the time that pendulum clocks suffered from changes in temperature, and that the cause lay in the pendulum itself, usually a metal rod with a lead bob on the end. The speed of a pendulum's swing varies with its length; to understand how this works, observe swings in a playground. The ones with long chains or ropes swing slowly, the ones with short chains or ropes swing faster. Whether a swing is carrying one, two, or no children, the time it takes to go from one extreme to the other depends on the length of its rope.

Pendulums behave like swings—their speed is controlled by their length. But because metals are affected by temperature, the length of a metal rod is never fixed and changeless. The warmth of summer makes the metal expand, so that the rod grows longer. In winter the opposite happens: the metal contracts from the cold and the rod grows shorter. These are extremely small changes, but enough to make a clock speed up in winter and slow down in summer. Clock-makers knew all about it; what they didn't know was how to fix it.

The remedy John Harrison invented began with a series of experiments described in his manuscript of 1730. He knew that different metals contract or expand at slightly different rates. If he could make a pendulum out of two kinds of metal rods, alternating with each other and lightly pinned together, then the contraction of one metal should compensate for the contraction of the other. But which metals?

To find out, he built some sort of shed—he calls it a Convenience—"on the outside of the Wall of my House, where the sun at 1 or 2 a Clock makes it very warm." The rods were kept in the shed so their expansion rates could be measured and compared, both in the cool of the evening and by the heat of day. He wanted two metals with substantially different rates, and he compared steel with iron, brass, silver, and copper, finally settling on steel and brass. Nine slender rods, steel alternating with brass, became what he called his gridiron pendulum. The device was so successful that an altered form of it remains in use today.

To have noticed that different metals have different expansion rates was a remarkable thing. Far more remarkable was what followed: finding a way of measuring them, then doing it with accuracy, and then making use of what was learned from the accurate measurements. It was a form of experimental metallurgy, perhaps, or else solid-state physics. In John Harrison's lifetime, there were no words for what he was doing.

Other inventions in the new clocks reduced friction to a minimum; there was a kind of "roller bearing," for example, as well as the anti-friction wheels made of lignum vitae. Harrison had also created a new type of escapement. Efficient and almost frictionless, it came to be known as the grasshopper escapement because of a "kicking" motion made by the long pallet arm when released by the escape wheel.

The two new pendulum clocks, with their gridirons, their rust-free, oil-free wooden innards, and their ingenious grasshopper escapements, were worked and reworked, taken apart repeatedly and repeatedly put back together, for several years. By 1726, John was ready to adjust them—meaning, to ensure that they were accurate over long periods.

Again, we have the 1730 manuscript. To adjust the clocks, he was going to need a standard of some sort—a precision timekeeper, the kind called a regulator. There was no such clock in Lincolnshire, however, and there was no one to advise him about how to get one elsewhere in England; except for James, he was entirely on his own.

Still on his own except for James, he found a timekeeper in the night skies over Barrow. Standing by a kitchen window, keeping in view the edge of its window frame, he observed the fraction of a second when a certain star disappeared behind a neighbor's chimney—

the moment "by which the Rays of a Star are taken from my sight almost in an instant," as the manuscript has it. The clocks were being tested against star time—scientists call it sidereal time—night after night, adjusted, tested, and tested again, until the brothers found they were accurate to within a second a month.

A second a month was better than the best timekeepers made by the finest craftsmen in London. Yet these clocks had been made by two country carpenters in a place so isolated the outside world barely knew it existed. No one advised or encouraged them, and they had no resources beyond the handmade tools of their carpentry shop. All the same, the clocks were marvels. John Harrison was prepared to say so to anyone who would listen.

2

A REVOLUTION IN MAPMAKING

he possibility that longitude could be learned from a clock was not new. In 1714, when the great prize was first proposed, Sir Isaac Newton delivered a statement on the subject: "That, for determining the Longitude at Sea, there have been several Projects, true in Theory, but difficult to execute . . . One is, by a Watch to keep time exactly: But, by reason of the Motion of a Ship, the Variation of Heat and Cold, Wet and Dry, and the Difference of Gravity in Different Latitudes, such a Watch hath not yet been made."

The Board of Longitude had been offered a number of schemes for sea clocks, but none of them was going to survive wild weather. The most accurate timekeepers had pendulums, and even the ordinary rocking of a ship sent them into uncontrolled swings, after which several days on land were needed to restore them to health. Watches, using the balance wheel instead of the pendulum, were not known for accuracy. And yet the project was true in theory: difficult to execute, but theoretically possible once the nature of longitude is understood.

In order to imagine lines of longitude that section the earth from pole to pole, it is first necessary to know the earth is a globe. Pythagoras, in the sixth century B.C., decided it was, probably because he'd watched ships disappear over the horizon. People began trying to estimate the size of this globe. In the third century B.C., a Greek named Eratosthenes did so; by means of a fiery intellect, focused on geometrical analysis of the sun's shadow, he calculated the distance around its middle as 25,000 miles. His methods were essentially the same as those in use today, and the result today is the same: 24,901 miles.

Because the earth was now seen as a globe, it could be divided into halves, one part being north of the midsection, the other part south. In the second century A.D., Claudius Ptolemy, a Greek, published an eight-volume *Geography* in which the earth was marked by lines parallel to the equator—the latitudes—and lengthwise—from pole to pole—by lines of longitude. His sense of the Mediterranean and its coasts was remarkably accurate; this was his own backyard, after all, and well explored. But the rest of his world was vague, and in the centuries that followed there was no improvement—if anything, the accuracy of maps declined.

With Gutenberg's invention of printing, not many years before Columbus set off toward the Americas, it became possible to replace handmade maps with printed ones. Brilliantly hand-colored, sometimes with highlights of liquid gold or silver, they contained vast amounts of misinformation, but were both cheaper and easier to come by than earlier maps. All the publishers needed now was good maps to copy, and they were desperately needed.

There had been a wealth of discoveries in the New World; as a consequence, European monarchs held claims in many foreign lands. Yet none of them could locate what he claimed. No one could say where the new places fitted in with the old, and nobody knew the dimensions of the great sea that separated Europe from the Americas.

It was not until the seventeenth century that the art of mapmaking became a science. The transformation started far from Earth, in the icy darkness of interplanetary space. The Italian physicist and astronomer Galileo, improving on an earlier invention, developed a powerful astronomical telescope. With its help he made an extraordinary discovery, one that could be used as a kind of celestial clock. The planet Jupiter, he found, was orbited by four moons invisible to the naked eye. These four moons circle around Jupiter in stately procession, now appearing, now disappearing behind the planet. And Jupiter is far enough away from Earth so that it can be seen from any place on Earth. This is what makes it a celestial clock. The moons are its hands.

In 1612 Galileo drew up tables showing the positions of the moons at various hours of the night, tables that could be prepared several months in advance and used to tell the time at two different places at once. This development was crucial to knowledge of longitude, which translates space into time, as follows:

The globe that is the earth is divided, by convention, into 360 sections. Picture them as resembling a thinly sliced apple. The lines that separate the slices, or sections, are the longitudes, also called meridians. Stretching from pole to pole, they pass through the equator on the way.

As the earth rotates on its axis, it makes a complete, 360-degree rotation every twenty-four hours. This means 15 degrees in an hour, or one degree every four minutes.

Therefore each of the sections has a turn being opposite the sun, so that from the time one section passes the sun until the next section passes, four minutes will have gone by. With every degree of longitude we travel westward, then, local noon is four minutes later. And for every degree of longitude we travel eastward, local noon is four minutes sooner. So finding the longitude is simply a matter of knowing the time in two places at once. As soon as Galileo gave the world the celestial clock, it became possible to do just that.

In the late seventeenth century, when modern mapmaking began, France was the first nation to set up an organized, science-based mapping project. Expeditions planned by its Academy of Sciences fanned out across the Western Hemisphere, equipped with instruments and charts. Having reached a destination—Guadeloupe, for instance—the French astronomers would find a level space on land and set up their instruments. By "shooting the sun," observing the sun's midday height above the horizon, they determined their latitude, as well as exact local time. This was done with the aid of a quadrant, and by consulting tables that gave corrections for the sun's seasonal movements—higher in summer, lower in winter.

The method was much the same as the one used by the ancients. The tables had existed for centuries, and the quadrant was a direct descendant of the astrolabe. But our mapmaking astronomers in Guadeloupe had something unknown to the ancient world, namely, the telescope. At night, they used it to monitor the comings and goings of Jupiter's moons. By comparing what they saw through the lens with the charts they had brought from home, they learned what time it was in Paris. They had already found exact local time; now the difference between Paris time and Guadeloupe time gave them their longitude.

Expeditions of this sort, sponsored by the great powers of Europe, were gradually transforming the map and the globe, fixing international boundaries, locating remote islands by pinning them to a longitude and latitude. And it was Jupiter's moons—the celestial

clock—that made this possible, finding longitude by telling time in two places at once.

But the celestial clock did nothing whatever for navigators. Observing the moons of Jupiter meant focusing a primitive telescope on a tiny point of light in the sky, which was difficult enough on land, and out of the question with a ship's deck quaking underfoot. For the sailor, nothing had changed. Longitude was still his mortal enemy.

Yet Harrison believed he could capture longitude and the prize with a seagoing clock. Not just a clock that would work at sea but one that would do so with precision—that was the key word, precision. According to the terms of the prize, the device, or invention, must survive a voyage to the West Indies, meaning a trial at sea of about six weeks. And at journey's end it must show the longitude of the port of arrival to within half a degree of longitude, which translates to two minutes of time.

To see how this works, take an error of three seconds a day, and multiply by six weeks, or forty days. It adds up to exactly two minutes, so that on a voyage from England to the Caribbean a prize-winning clock would have to be accurate to three seconds a day. This was clearly impossible, since the best clocks were pendulum clocks and could function at sea only in a dead calm.

Harrison had something different in mind, something described in his 1730 manuscript. He wanted a clock without a pendulum in the usual sense. In its place would be a set of oscillating bars controlled by coiled springs, self-contained, and counterbalanced so as to survive the ship's motions. No such clock had ever existed. Perhaps nobody had even imagined such a clock. And if Harrison had served an apprenticeship in the usual way, learning from a master, he might not have imagined it either; he would have learned whatever the master had to teach, he would have done what he was taught and done it well, and made a very good living at it—without risk, without the danger of failure. Without being compelled to think along new and unconventional lines.

Now he had to consider what his family and James's family would do for money while they were building this clock. To succeed at sea, it must be sturdier than the wooden clocks, which meant many of the parts would have to be made of brass. They would need to hire experienced metal craftsmen, another expense. He hoped the Board of Longitude, if approached the right way, would give him something in the way of a loan or a grant—not much, since the Harrison families lived very simply. But they couldn't live on air.

The 1730 manuscript, twenty-two pages long, sets out all his recent work—how he had "in these 3 last Years . . . brought a Clock to go nearer the truth, than can be well imagin'd, considering the vast Number of seconds of Time there is in a Month, in which space of time, it does not vary above one second . . . so that I am sure I can bring it to the Nicety of 2 or 3 seconds in a Year. And 'twill also continue this exactness for 40 or 50 years or more."

Knowing that the great men he hoped to see might not believe such a claim, he included diagrams of his gridiron pendulum and other inventions in order to persuade them. Nevertheless, they might be impressed by his inventions, and still refuse to believe he could produce a sea clock. And suppose they refused to see him in the first place—suppose he never had a chance to present his claims, his diagrams, his request for a loan?

They were busy and important men with resounding titles. According to the Longitude Act, which first created this Board of Longitude, it was to consist of the Astronomer Royal; the President of the Royal Society; the Speaker of the House of Commons; the Master of Trinity House; the First Commissioner of the Navy; the First Commissioner of Trade; the Lord High Admiral; the Admirals of the Red, White, and Blue Squadrons; three professors of mathematics from Oxford and Cambridge; and ten members of Parliament.

This distinguished company had already received proposals. Most were sent by swindlers and fools, who often submitted at the same time their plans for squaring the circle, or for building perpetual-motion machines. Newspapers used the phrase "finding the longitude" to mean a search for the impossible. Worse than impossible —there was a hint of lunacy in it. The artist William Hogarth, in his paintings of *The Rake's Progress*, shows a madhouse scene with naked inmates writhing on a bare floor, while a madman scribbles on the wall his calculations for finding longitude at sea. By 1730, nothing of value had ever been presented to the Board.

Harrison's manuscript was made up of twenty-nine sections, the first twenty-four describing his precision clocks, the last five devoted to the proposed "Sea Clock." There was a good deal of detail in those last five sections, but much had been left out, for patent law was still in its infancy, and Harrison was afraid of having his ideas stolen. Also, the manuscript was written in a curious style. John Harrison could explain his ideas out loud with perfect clarity, but once he put pen to paper he began a kind of stuttering, repeating and qualifying and contradicting himself, until his meaning lay buried beneath a pileup of parentheses. This trait grew worse with age. Toward the end of his life he put together a pamphlet whose opening sentence took up twenty-five nearly unpunctuated pages, after which it stopped. Abruptly. For no apparent reason.

Unaware of this handicap, he signed his 1730 manuscript in a large, flourishing hand with outsize capital letters. The pride he took in his work shows in the signature. He believed in his clocks; his belief in them was passionate and unshakable—otherwise he would never have taken so daring a step as a trip to London, a place unknown to him, impossible for him to picture or even imagine. Then he left his wife and infant son with James, and set out.

3

INTO THE GREAT WORLD

ondon was nearly two hundred miles away, which meant a long and wretchedly uncomfortable journey by stagecoach. The roads were unpaved, uncared-for, in such desperate condition during the winter months that wagons and loaded packhorses regularly bogged down in muddy stretches. Bands of armed robbers swarmed the highway with no one to stop them, no troops, patrol, or police. Wayside inns, where travelers had to stay the night, were infested by lice and vermin, and the same was true of London. In the early years of the eighteenth century it was a filthy, brutal, dangerous place.

Londoners considered it the absolute center of the universe, the only city worth living in, attracting everyone who mattered. A man like John Harrison, in rough homespun clothing, his sturdy shoes made by a village cobbler, did not matter. Such men could be seized upon by a London mob and ridiculed, turned this way and that, their hats pulled off and tossed into the gutter that overflowed with the emptyings of chamber pots and the droppings of horses. Tradesmen, including butchers, used the gutter as their lawful dumping grounds. It was an open and stinking sewer.

London people seemed to live and die in these streets. Shopkeepers standing outside their doors invited passersby to come inside and get drunk for a penny or dead drunk for twopence. Bullbaitings, cockfights, and public hangings were popular with citizens of all classes, servants and masters. In the two-room hovels of the poor, where people lived eight or ten to a room, pigs and chickens inhabited the cellars. Only a quarter of London-born babies survived their infancy. There were no city police, no streetlights, no public education. The poor had no political rights at all, and nobody seemed to think they deserved or needed them.

But if London was poor, London was also dazzlingly rich. The great cities of Europe had nothing to compare with the glamour of her finest shops. Merchant princes—the heads of such enterprises as the East India Company—had transformed the capital into a marketplace for luxury goods. From wharves and docks along the Thames, British-owned vessels sailed to Venice, Macao, America. They carried homegrown products such as textiles and brought back tobacco, sugar, coffee, tea, chocolate, spices, Chinese porcelain, cashmere shawls, furs from the snowy forests of North America, and black slaves. Much of what they brought back was reexported and sold abroad. All of it created wealth.

The comings and goings of ships had another meaning. Those who could afford it were increasingly eager to know the rest of the world. On the Continent, they searched out whatever was new and practical: different methods of farming, different fruits, vegetables, crafts, dyes, styles of architecture, and, above all, new ideas. It was an age of intellectual excitement. Political and religious experiment blossomed. Science was rapidly becoming an international language that crossed all boundaries.

The English were an island nation, and shipping was their lifeblood, also the source of their prestige, their status among the nations, their pride in Englishness. So it is understandable that the prize offered by the British Parliament, the one that had lured John Harrison to London, should be richer and more famous than the prizes offered by competing countries, all of them desperate for a solution to longitude.

Whatever Harrison thought and felt when he first saw this great city can only be guessed at, just as his plan for presenting himself to one or more members of the Board of Longitude is left to the imagination. But we know that he succeeded. Somehow or other he managed to meet Edmond Halley, who was the King's Astronomer Royal, and an influential member of the Board. Halley lived and worked in the Greenwich Observatory, which was on the highest ground in Greenwich Park, close to the Thames River.

What Harrison found when he got there was a man in his mid-seventies, tall, thin, nearly toothless, although very much alert. He was one of the great scientists of his era, having made contributions to mathematics and physics as well as astronomy; he had a colorful past and broad interests.

At the age of twenty Halley had dropped out of Oxford and set sail for the island of St. Helena, in the South Atlantic Ocean, where he spent over a year mapping the stars of the Southern Hemisphere. In later life he became a deep-sea diver for a while, designed a diving bell, and managed an undersea salvage operation. He was befriended by Russia's Peter the Great, who came to England to learn ship-building and worked with his own hands at the Royal Dock. The Czar knew Halley by reputation and asked to meet him; they became drinking companions.

Harrison describes his interview with the Astronomer Royal in a manuscript he wrote toward the end of his life, in 1775, and from it we can gather that Halley listened while Harrison talked—and talked and talked, carried away by his pride in the splendidly accurate clocks he had built, and the one he longed to make with the help of the Board.

But Halley was convinced that longitude at sea would never be found with a clock, not even the splendidly accurate one Harrison described. It would be found by astronomical means, probably with a

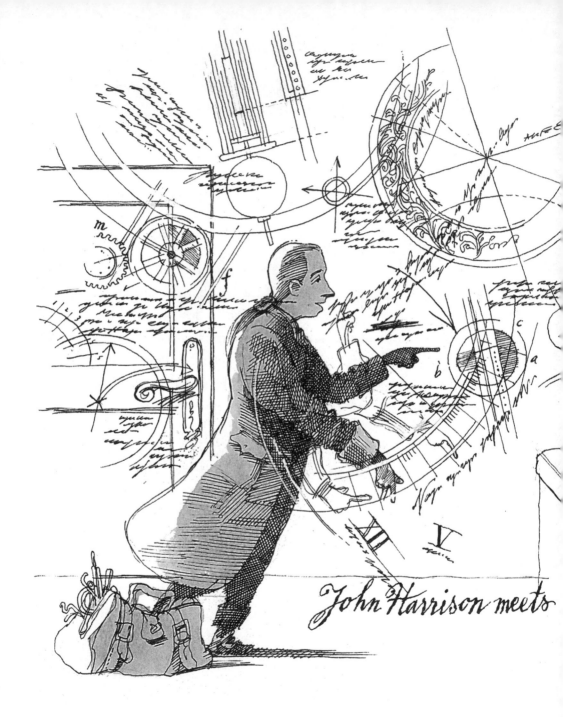

John Harrison meets

Edmond Halley

system that predicted movements of the moon. He had been working on such a system for many years.

All the same, when his young visitor had finally talked himself out, Halley offered encouragement. Maybe he was something of a gambler. Maybe it was simply a matter of fair-mindedness. According to Harrison's account, Halley told him: What you ought to do is go to see George Graham. He explained that while Graham was not a member of the Board, he was a Fellow of the Royal Society, an expert on the design of scientific instruments, and the country's most eminent clockmaker.

No, that wouldn't do at all, Harrison said. Out of the question. As the 1775 manuscript explains his feelings, the older man's advice "went hard with me, for I thought it as a Step very improper to be taken." Suppose Graham, the clockmaker, pirated his ideas?

Halley replied that since the Board knew nothing about clocks they would certainly send him to Graham in any case, and he might as well go on his own. Halley also told him that "Mr. Graham was . . . very honest . . . and would do me no harm, viz. as by pirating any Thing from me, but that on the contrary, would certainly do me Good if it was in his Power."

By way of further encouragement, Halley offered to write a letter of introduction to Graham, and he also offered some advice. Be tactful, he said, when presenting your ideas to Graham. And be brief.

Although Harrison remembered those words, it's not likely that he listened to them. It wasn't in him to listen. Halley was a gentleman, so was Graham, and tact would be important to them, as would the social graces in general. But Harrison had no social graces whatever; he was blunt, outspoken, easily angered. We know this from the tone of his pamphlets and writings, just as we know he was without pretense of any kind, also down-to-earth, truthful, and modest about his own accomplishments.

Halley wrote the letter, and not long afterward John Harrison came to Graham's house one day at ten in the morning. He must have been in a combative mood, for in the same 1775 narrative he tells us that Graham "began, as I thought it, very roughly with me . . . which had like to have occasioned me to become rough too; but however, we got the Ice broke."

The gridiron pendulum was surely the icebreaker, for Graham had tried fifteen years earlier to make a pendulum along the same lines. He never succeeded. Now he had before him an uneducated man from an unknown village who said he had made exactly such a pendulum. He had made clocks, he said, that kept time to within a second a month—an astonishing claim. Graham's own clocks, the finest available, were not nearly so good. Furthermore, Harrison was some twenty years younger, with decades of working life ahead of him.

Graham could have been jealous of all this talent and energy. Instead, he was delighted. As Harrison recalls, "he became as at last vastly surprised at the Thoughts or Methods I had taken, or had found Occasion to take, and as thence found Reason enough to believe that my Clock might go to a Second a Month."

Graham was eager to hear everything, to go through the manuscript page by page until all the diagrams were fully explained. While apprentices came and went, the two men huddled in the room, head to head, talking and reasoning, as Harrison tells us, "from about Ten o'clock in the Forenoon till about Eight at Night, the Time which Dinner took up included, for he invited me to stay to dine."

From that day forward, George Graham was a loyal supporter of all John Harrison's works. He advised against any approach to the Board at this point, saying it would be best to return to Barrow, build the sea clock, and when it was finished bring it to London. As for the money, he made a loan from his own pocket—most accounts guess it was some two hundred pounds—with never a word about security or interest. For Harrison, this was the start of an invaluable friendship.

He tells us nothing about the journey home, so we can only speculate about his thoughts, which were probably mixed. He had been received with kindness by two important men, yet he never met the all-powerful Board of Longitude. He had money, but hardly enough to support two families for several years, which meant that he and James would have to build the clock in whatever free time they could snatch from work. James might find this discouraging. John was probably looking forward to the struggle.

And in Philadelphia, on the other side of the ocean whose dimensions nobody knew for certain, Thomas Godfrey, the glazier, had already completed his invention. It was a new form of quadrant that John Hadley of Hertfordshire invented at about the same time. This instrument was the first useful result of the Longitude Act, and it was going to revolutionize nautical astronomy.

Earlier quadrants, such as cross-staff and backstaff, were designed to find the latitude and local time by gauging the height of the sun, or a particular star, above the horizon. They were tricky to use aboard ship, not especially accurate, and impossible in rough weather.

The Godfrey-Hadley instruments were reflecting quadrants, based on paired mirrors so that the sun and the sea's horizon could be seen simultaneously; even with a ship's deck rocking underfoot, it was possible now to make precise measurements for latitude. But neither Godfrey nor Hadley was primarily interested in latitude. Longitude was what they were after. And with the new quadrant it became possible to measure the elevations of two celestial bodies, as well as the distance between them; therefore positions of the moon could be measured in relation to some designated star— easily, accurately. And with that the lunar system for longitude, the one that Edmond Halley and most of the Board believed in—that the immortal Isaac Newton had believed in—jumped one step closer to reality.

In 1732 a description of the reflecting quadrant was sent to Halley by James Logan, Chief Justice of Pennsylvania's Supreme Court, and a good friend of Godfrey's. After describing the new instrument— Godfrey called it his theodolite—Logan says, "And if the method of

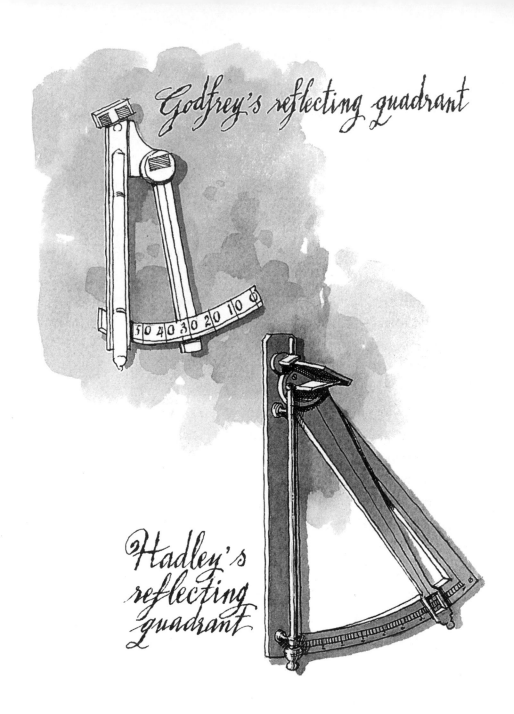

Godfrey's reflecting quadrant

Hadley's reflecting quadrant

discovering the longitude by the moon is to meet with a reward, and this instrument . . . be made use of, in that case I would recommend the inventor to thy justice and notice."

The inventor, as it happened, was a neighbor of Benjamin Franklin, who leaves a capsule portrait of him in the famous autobiography. We learn that Godfrey belonged to the Junto Club, a society Franklin had organized for others like himself, young workingmen interested in self-improvement. And according to Franklin, Godfrey "was not a pleasing companion; as, like most great mathematicians I have met with, he expected universal precision in everything said, and was for ever denying or distinguishing upon trifles, to the disturbance of all conversation."

Logan's letter to Halley was never answered; maybe it was never received. Two years passed. Then, in 1734, Godfrey learned that the Royal Society was about to reward its vice president, John Hadley, for an invention similar to the theodolite. Once more Godfrey turned to Justice Logan. Logan collected affidavits about the history of Godfrey's device, including accounts of its sea trials as early as 1730, and sent them to the Astronomer Royal, hoping they would establish Godfrey's priority.

But John Hadley had already established priority. He was a Hertfordshire landowner, whose interest in optics brought him to the attention of the Royal Society, a group of scientists serving as semi-official advisers to the government; in the summer of 1731 their journal, *Philosophical Transactions*, published a description of his new instrument. It was a distinguished publication, read also by Europeans and Americans, and simply by appearing in its pages John Hadley became the recognized inventor of the reflecting quadrant. A few years later, he took out a patent on it.

The scientific community could have shared the credit equally between both men, but it didn't happen that way. From the start, the new instrument was known as Hadley's quadrant. It has never been called anything else, certainly not theodolite.

Hadley's quadrant evolved into the sextant and is in use even today. But Godfrey died comparatively young, unknown, and almost unremembered. At the time of his death, the method for discovering longitude by the moon was still elusive, the great difficulty being that the moon's movements were too complex to be predicted. And when the moon's secrets were finally captured, when the Board of Longitude had all the pieces of the puzzle within its grasp, even Hadley was dead. Neither Hadley nor Godfrey had any part of the longitude prize because they were some twenty-five years ahead of their time.

All the same, by the early 1730s the reflecting quadrant, the first significant step in the creation of a lunar system, very solidly existed. And John Harrison's sea clock, which represented the only other possibility for measuring longitude at sea, was slowly coming to life in Barrow.

Nothing whatever is known about this period in the lives of the Harrison brothers. They simply disappear for four years, and reappear at the end of that time with a clock, one that can be seen today in the National Maritime Museum at Greenwich. Lovingly restored, it looks now as it did then—unlike any other clock, and very much like a ship, high-masted although without sails, and armed with fantasy weapons that stick out at curious angles.

The clock is 2 feet high, a little more than 2 feet wide, and 16½ inches deep, and weighs 75 pounds. Although spring-driven, like the watches of Harrison's day, it does not function like a watch. Except for the escapement, its wheelworks are made of oak, and everything else is metal, mostly brass.

In place of a pendulum there are two large brass balances, each with a brass ball at either end—dumbbell balances. Linked by springs, the balls swing together, then swing apart, then together again, beating out the seconds in perfect unison. When the clock is tilted or turned, the regularity of its balances is undisturbed, since any effect produced on one set of balances is counteracted by an equal movement of the other set. The clock was so designed that, during rewinding, it neither stops nor slows. On its face are four dials wreathed by eight carved cherubs and four crowns; the dials show seconds, minutes, hours, and days of the month. Harrison's Number One—H-1, as it came to be called—was the first accurate and portable clock ever made.

He had it mounted in gimbals, a suspension system designed so that the object suspended remains level no matter how its frame is tilted. The clock and the suspension system were then placed inside

Harrison's H-1

a large wooden case that was further suspended by spiral springs at the corners, and taken aboard a barge in the Humber River. The Harrison brothers tested it extensively on the Humber—we know this from a statement John made some years later to the Royal Society. And when they were finally satisfied with its performance, in 1735, John took it to London so it could be given a sea trial by the Board of Longitude. He never tells us how he got it there, but it is generally believed that he took the clock apart and traveled overland with it.

What happened next has to be pieced together out of suppositions. It's likely that Harrison got in touch with George Graham and Edmond Halley, and that those two steadfast friends did their best to alert the Board of Longitude. And that the Board had no idea how to respond, since it had been in existence for over twenty years without once holding a meeting.

Halley and Graham then turned to the Royal Society, and at least five of their fellow members inspected the sea clock. This is known by way of a certificate the five wrote out, stating their belief that the "Machine for measuring time at sea . . . highly deserves Public Encouragement."

Perhaps the Royal Society also prodded the Admiralty. Yet it wasn't until May of the following year that Harrison was told to take the clock to Spithead, where he would board HMS *Centurion* and sail with the clock to Lisbon, Portugal. It would be a trial at sea, sponsored by the Royal Society rather than the Board of Longitude, therefore unofficial and informal—but a sea trial all the same. Our evidence is a letter from Sir Charles Wager, First Lord of the Admiralty, to *Centurion's* Captain Proctor: "The Instrument . . . has been approved by all the Mathematicians in Town that have seen it (and few have not) to be the Best that has been made for measuring Time: how it will succeed at Sea, you will partly be a Judge . . . The Man is said by those who know him best to be a very ingenious and sober Man, and capable of finding out something more than he has already, if he can find Encouragement."

In his letter of reply, Captain Proctor assured Sir Charles that he would do everything in his power to help: "I find him to be a very sober, a very industrious, and withal a very modest Man . . . but the Difficulty of measuring Time truly, where so many unequal Shocks, and Motions, stand in Opposition to it, gives me concern . . . and makes me fear he has attempted Impossibilities."

Notice that both letters describe Mr. Harrison as a "Man." They think well of this Man, who is sober, industrious, and, in the captain's opinion, modest. But they do not describe him as a "Gentleman," since he isn't one. In eighteenth-century England the difference was unmistakable and of considerable importance.

So John Harrison took H-1 to Spithead. He leaves no report of anything that happened during the outward-bound voyage; we must assemble the picture from what is generally known about the Royal Navy during that era. There is one exception, the ship itself. A good deal is known about HMS *Centurion* through accounts of a long and dangerous voyage she made, but that was several years in the future. For the time being, we can be sure only that the clockmaker and his clock were taken aboard the captain's barge, which served to ferry important passengers from land to wherever the ship lay at anchor. Although the pair of them might not look important, the bargemen must have known they were—for inside the box was a device they had heard about, a watch-machine for finding the longitude, one that might save thousands of common sailors from death by shipwreck.

It would save officers as well, but officers were in the navy because they wanted to be. Jack Tar, the ordinary sailor, was not necessarily consulted about joining the navy—was often knocked on the head in some dark alley, beaten, shoved, and finally thrown aboard. Death by shipwreck was only one of the mortal dangers he had to face.

4

ABOARD HMS *CENTURION*

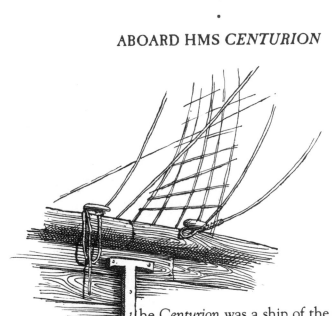

The *Centurion* was a ship of the line, a specialist fighting ship mounting sixty guns, almost half of them twenty-four-pounders capable of smashing through a ship's side. Although not the largest of her kind, she was nevertheless a seagoing fortress, and when fully outfitted carried four hundred men. Her current orders were to join the main fleet at Lisbon, a voyage that could be made in a week if the winds behaved; once in Lisbon, Harrison and his clock were to be put ashore until some other ship could be found to bring them home.

For the crew, the journey that lay ahead would be routine—short, safe, predictable. For Harrison, nothing about it could have been routine, every step from the first lowering of H-1 into the barge a possible source of danger. Once safely aboard, his clock must endure the shocks of the ship's motions, the changes in temperature, in moisture and dryness, the storms that might spring up suddenly and without warning, flooding the deck and the clock along with it, with the crew too busy to give a thought to its welfare. Although H-1 had been tested on river barges, it had never been aboard an oceangoing vessel; neither had Harrison.

We have no way of knowing what quarters he was assigned to, but H-1 was "placed in my Cabbin," as Captain Proctor informed Sir Charles Wager, to give Harrison "all the Advantage that is possible for making his Observations." Other things were being taken aboard at the same time, the usual supplies from the Admiralty storehouse that equipped Royal Navy ships of Harrison's era—barrels of rope, nails, canvas, candles, also barrels of hardtack, salt pork, and salt beef. Five days a week, the cook was going to hack off chunks of this meat and pass them out to the common sailors; on the other two days it would be hacked-off chunks of salted fish and cheese. All were accompanied by ship's biscuit. Unappetizing to begin with, by the end of a voyage this dense, gray, cement-like bread was usually crawling with weevils.

Provisions for the officers' meals, purchased by the officers themselves, were taken aboard at the same time, and included coops filled

Embarking on a trial at sea

with chickens to ensure a supply of eggs and fresh meat. There might be sheep, cows, and pigs as well, although these were more usual on longer voyages; sometimes a goat was taken aboard so the officers could have fresh milk. Senior officers brought their own cooks, as did the captain, who had a dining room of his own.

Sailors and officers climbed rope ladders to the main deck, along with the personal servants of the officers. As for Jack Tar—the nickname was probably short for "tarpaulin"—he went down after that. Not so far down as the hold where the cargo was kept, rotting and leaking into the bilgewater, but to a space between the hold and the main deck. Aboard the *Centurion*, hundreds of ordinary sailors shared this area with the cannons, since it served as the gun deck, and with their dining tables, since they ate there. At night they unrolled their hammocks, tied them to stanchions, the upright bars supporting the deck overhead, and went to sleep—wearing the same clothes they had worn all day, wet or dry, for they had no others. In this dark, damp, foul-smelling area the hammocks were crowded together, some higher, some lower, one man's feet beside another man's head, each of them occupying a space about fourteen or fifteen inches wide.

Their officers had chosen the navy because it was a gentlemanly occupation, as well as an adventurous one. In wartime, they stood a chance of earning promotion and medals, and prize money for any enemy ship they helped capture, so they welcomed war. But for Jack Tar there was a different set of rules. The thugs who swept the back alleys for men to kidnap and throw aboard were called press-gangs, and functioned as unofficial arms of the navy. In times of war, it was typical for half the men aboard ship to be pressed men, captured from jail cells, hospitals, even old sailors' homes.

Whether they were washed overboard in heavy seas, fell from the higher ropes of the rigging, or were caught by enemy fire in combat, maiming and death were commonplace for ordinary sailors. Their injuries were handled in sick bay, a miserable hole without sanitary facilities. Their appalling diet weakened them, leaving them easy prey for scurvy, a wholesale killer of sailors. They could be flogged on their bare backs with the cat-o'-nine-tails at the whim of their superiors, or hanged from the yardarm for rebellious behavior. They worked, they were there to work, would not be fed unless they did work. But officers never worked, for there was a strong tradition in the navy as well as the army against officers doing work of any kind; their job was giving orders. Similarly, high-ranking officers did not speak to sailors; the captain's orders, for example, were relayed to the bosun, who piped them out for the sailors. Even junior officers did not speak directly to the captain if they could help it. They spoke to the Almighty when saying their prayers, but with the captain they waited to be spoken to. What ordinary sailors did if they happened to cross the captain's path was get out of it fast. They were the wretched of the earth, human flotsam, sometimes criminals, sometimes simply poor and powerless. To stay alive they had to work together, each man depending on his neighbor, tied as surely to him as ropes were tied to canvas, and the Royal Navy would have been nothing without this community of comrades. Along with the winds and the sails, they were the engine that powered its ships in the years of its greatest glory.

We cannot suppose that the novelties of shipboard life—the bells, the bosun's piping, the tattoo of drumbeats announcing the officers' meals—were likely to make much of an impression on John Harrison. A man who has devoted four years to the building of one instrument is not easily distracted. True, the purpose of the instrument was to save the lives of sailors; he knew it just as they knew it. But single-mindedness was one of the central themes of his character, and his energies would have been entirely focused on the care and maintenance of his beloved clock.

Harrison has left no record of its performance on the voyage to Lisbon; we know only that it took a week to get there. And the captain's log is no help, since Captain Proctor died soon after their arrival, without ever having written up his log. The *Centurion* was then given a new captain, George Anson, who took her to the Mediterranean, where she joined the main fleet; Harrison stayed in Lisbon with H-1, awaiting further orders.

Four days later they were on their way home aboard HMS *Orford*, and at last we have news of them. According to the master's log, the weather was very mixed, gales alternating with calms, so many gales and calms that the voyage home lasted nearly a month. But H-1, untroubled by weather or changes in temperature, beat out the minutes as faithfully as it had in Harrison's workshop.

During the third week, when land was sighted near the entrance to the Channel—they were not far from the place where Sir Clowdisley Shovell and his ships went down almost thirty years earlier—people began to argue about their position. The master recorded in his log that "the said Land, according to my reckoning, and others, ought to have been the Start," a rocky headland in Devon. But before they knew what land it was, "John Harrison declared to me, and the rest of the Ship's Company, that according to his Observations with his Machine, it ought to be the Lizzard [another headland], the which indeed it was found to be, his Observations shewing the Ship to be more West, than my Reckoning." It was over sixty miles more west.

The master made out a certificate describing Harrison's prediction and how it proved to be right—the first time a professional navigator acknowledged that a clumsy, oversize machine-in-a-box could outdo dead reckoning.

This was not an official trial, since it had not been a voyage to the Indies, and its sponsor was the Royal Society rather than the Board of Longitude. Furthermore, the voyage was mostly due south and due north, with no great changes in longitude to test the clock's ability—even though the ship's master, making a routine journey, was wrong by more than sixty miles.

But Harrison had seen that his watch-machine could deal with the pitching and rolling, the violent shocks, and the sudden temperature changes of an oceangoing vessel. This should have been immensely satisfying to him. Yet it wasn't, at any rate not for long.

In June of 1737 the Board of Longitude met for the first time in its twenty-three-year history, and John Harrison came before it.

5

THE MIGHTY BOARD OF LONGITUDE

ccording to the minutes of the meeting only eight members were present, but Halley was there, and others Harrison had met through the Royal Society. The minutes also tell us that Harrison brought with him "a new invented Machine, in the nature of a Clock Work whereby he proposes to keep time at Sea with more exactness than by any other Instrument or method." He had brought the certificate given him by the master of the *Orford*, and both clock and certificate were examined by the gentlemen of the Board.

But then the minutes reveal a curious thing. It seems Harrison had not requested an official trial at sea, one sponsored by the Board of Longitude, that would qualify H-1 for the prize. What Harrison wanted was a modest grant of money so that he could "make another machine of smaller dimensions within the space of two years."

Apparently he had already started work on this other machine, but could not finish it without something to live on. And why had he turned away from the first clock after it gave such a promising performance? Because he wanted to "correct some defects which he hath found [in it] . . . so as to render the same more perfect."

The nature of these defects is unknown. Most accounts maintain that even with the defects, whatever they were, H-1 would have qualified for one of the lesser prizes. But a lesser prize was not what Harrison had in mind. If they would grant him the sum of 500 pounds, he said, he would be able to finish this second machine in which the faults of the first would be corrected, and then, only then, would he be ready for a trial at sea.

According to the minutes, the Board "examined and decided," and finally agreed that Harrison should have his grant, half to be paid at once, half when the second machine was put aboard a ship headed for the West Indies. And when that ship returned to England, both machines, the first and the second, were to become the property of the nation.

These were harsh terms. Surely they had no right to the first clock, which had been built entirely at Harrison's expense. And it's not clear that they had any right to the second, except if it should win the prize. Yet Harrison accepted their offer without argument. He was apparently under the impression that they were sponsoring him and the new clock, that he had been commissioned to build it, for when he finished H-2, he had it engraved with these words: "Made for His Majesty George the IInd By order of a Committee Held the 30th of June 1737."

And when the meeting of June 30 was over, he returned to Barrow, to get his family and James's ready for a permanent move to London. Maybe Graham and Halley had persuaded the brothers that it was important to live where there were wheel cutters, spring makers, and other craftsmen. We know they found lodgings and workshop space on a street called Leather Lane, but after that they disappeared once more into obscurity.

We see them again in 1739; by then they were living and working in Red Lion Square, and H-2 was finished. This second clock had certain refinements of detail, such as a greatly improved temperature compensation, and wheelworks made of brass. Otherwise its chief difference from H-1 was that it took up about half the space, an important feature from the viewpoint of any ship's captain who had to live with it.

According to a report by the Royal Society, during the next two years the clock was "agitated for many Hours together, with greater Violence than what it could receive from the Motion of a Ship in a Storm." The result, they said, was that H-2 was regular enough and

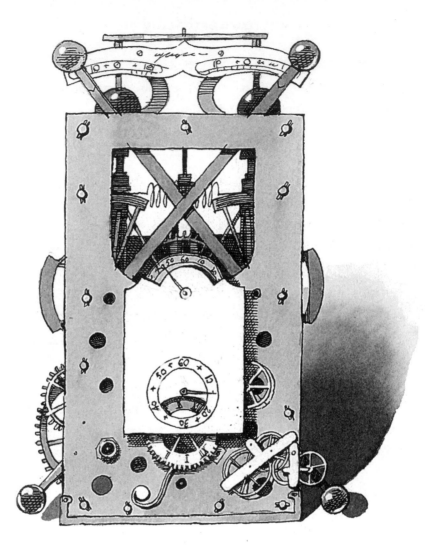

Harrison's H-2

exact enough to find longitude at sea "within the nearest Limits proposed by Parliament and probably much nearer."

But unlike the first clock, it was never tested at sea—possibly because war had broken out with Spain, and it was feared that the
clock might be captured. More likely the reason was John Harrison.
Again. He had discovered a defect in the balances, he said, "it happened by an accidental experiment," and while he might have over-
come this defect if he'd tried, he was unable to put his whole effort
into trying because he had fallen in love with a third machine. He
was already hard at work on it. Without waiting for funds or approval from the Board, and disregarding the thousands of hours he
had poured into H-2, he had chosen to follow another and brighter
dream.

Instead of the bar-shaped balances of the first two clocks, the balances of H-3 were circular, and he was full of hope for it, as he told
the Board. He needed only a small grant to live on while finishing it.
They gave him 500 pounds.

It was at some point during this period that the Harrison brothers'
partnership fell apart. The cause is unclear, but we know that James
left London and returned to the neighborhood of Barrow, where he
spent the rest of his life as a miller and bell caster. Maybe he had had
enough of their grubby existence, the pleading for money that was
doled out in driblets. Maybe he had had enough of John; not everyone can live indefinitely in the shadow of a brilliant older brother.

Now, for the first time in fifteen years, John was working entirely on his own. He told the Board the new clock would be ready for trial by the summer of 1743. Friends in the Royal Society encouraged him, and the Board released several more driblets of money. If John ever envied the normal life that James had chosen there is no sign of it, for he was doing what he most loved, his whole being engrossed in the task of perfecting a singular and beautiful object.

Yet 1743 came and went without the clock's being anywhere near completion. He had few other sources of income, he was working almost exclusively on this one project, but there it was: the clock resisted him. He said it was balky and temperamental, largely because of the new balances. Although he never once complained about this third and most difficult clock, he had reached the age of fifty. His son William, an infant when John first came to London, was already a teenager, old enough to help in the workshop. The years were piling up.

During those years a famous voyage took place, one that historians regularly cite as an example of the vital need for longitude at sea. HMS *Centurion* was its central character; others who figure in it appear again when the conflict between the watch-machine and the lunar-distance system for calculating longitude comes to a head. Richard Walter, who sailed with the expedition as chaplain, wrote about it in a narrative so richly detailed that we can see and smell its daily life—and death as well, for this is a death-haunted story.

It begins with a footnote to history: the war that had broken out with Spain, and was known as the War of Jenkins's Ear, after a British captain who lost his ship and one ear to the Spanish coast guard. The war's true cause was British hunger for commercial expansion. Bankers and laborers alike knew that meant greater prosperity, and everyone was greedy for greater prosperity; they were overjoyed once war was declared. It proved to be an expensive war, however, incompetently run, and inconclusive. The globe-circling journey made by Centurion was one of its few successes.

In 1739 the main British fleet was being readied to attack Spanish colonies in the Caribbean. As a secondary and background action, George Anson was to lead a squadron of six ships against Spanish holdings on the west coast of South America. He had joined the navy at fifteen and was now in his early forties, well born and well connected, his manner reserved but unassuming. Resolute and with a strong sense of duty, he must have had a strong stomach as well, for the outfitting of his squadron involved some of the Admiralty's most brutal decisions.

HMS Centurion had been Anson's ship for several years, since the death of Proctor, and she would serve as the expedition's flagship. She was in battered condition, however, crying out for total renovation, and the same was true of the five other, smaller ships. But the main fleet had stronger claims on English shipyards, and Anson would have to wait his turn. He needed fighting men as well as sailors—an entire regiment of marines, to make up the landing parties that would storm South American coastal towns. Promises were made, Anson was told to expect five hundred troops, but in the end the five hundred went elsewhere.

Another five hundred were promised, and this time the promise was partly kept. Two hundred fifty-nine arrived. All were pensioners from the Chelsea Hospital for retired soldiers—veterans of England's foreign wars who had been spending their sunset years in a nursing home. Most were over sixty, some over seventy, among them one-legged men, one-eyed men, and a few who were crazy. After straggling into Portsmouth to find their ships, some had to be carried aboard on stretchers. Two were so badly in need of medical attention that Anson had them sent to a Portsmouth hospital. When the Admiralty learned about it, both men were ordered out of the hospital and back aboard ship. They died within weeks. The question of how this pitiful troop of foot soldiers was supposed to harass the Spanish enemy has never been answered.

Meanwhile, major repairs to the ships were delayed or ignored. Press-gangs scoured the gutters of Portsmouth in search of fresh victims to join the crew. Barrels of trade goods to barter with the native peoples of the New World were taken aboard. They had to be fitted into the hold, and the hold was already densely packed with supplies for a long voyage, but the trade goods went in all the same. This meant that the sailors and the ancient foot soldiers had even less than their traditional fifteen inches—less space and air, in fact, than the cattle brought aboard as part of the officers' private food supply. In short, for his expedition against the Spanish strongholds of South

America, Anson was given six ships in broken-down condition with men to match.

After many delays, they set sail in the autumn of 1740, hoping to reach Cape Horn, the southernmost point of South America, by the following January. Apparently, Anson was not aware that the best time to round the Horn from the east was June or July. He was unprepared in other ways. The remedies he brought for scurvy—caused by a lack of vitamin C, which was unknown at the time—were Dr. Ward's drops and Dr. Ward's pills, both powerful laxatives. His charts and maps were the best available, made by Edmond Halley during expeditions to the South Atlantic, but that had been forty years earlier. And for finding the longitude, Anson had what every other seaman had, dead reckoning.

By November 1740, as they neared the equator, a scorching sun burned Centurion's upper deck. Belowdecks, her hold was a stinking caldron; more than ninety men had already died of fevers, dysentery, and scurvy. Anchored off the coast of Brazil for a time, they found fresh water and fruit, but in the sick tents seventy more died, many from tropical diseases carried by mosquitoes. In January 1741 they sailed for Patagonia, the deep cold of the southern seas, and Cape Horn.

George Anson had never made this voyage around the Horn, although a number of his men had, but every sailor knew its reputation. It was said that rounding the Horn in severe weather was the cruelest experience a man could be subjected to unless he were being punished for some hideous crime. Approaching it, they were met by snow flurries and hail, but no storms. Steep, snow-covered mountains surrounded them. The men put on oilskins if they had them, or tarred jackets, or wrapped themselves in old sails, with stockings pulled over their heads. Everyone talked about "westing," pushing west against the powerful eastward current, for the only way to beat that current and gain the Pacific coast was to make westing at all costs.

The squadron came through Le Maire Strait, a twenty-mile-wide channel considered the start of the journey around the Horn, in a couple of hours and in clear, bright weather. Then the sky darkened, black clouds blotted out the sun, and the wind changed. They were struck by a whining squall, sudden and violent, that stopped only long enough to give birth to new squalls. Great waves rolled across the ocean, some over sixty feet high, and the wind never stopped screaming.

Men were torn from the deck by the pitching motion of the ship and washed overboard, others were slammed to the deck, or thrown down into the hold, some killed, some crippled. Water invaded the ship and had to be pumped out, the pumps worked day and night by men who sometimes died at their posts. From below came an erratic noise of booming: the "heavy shot"—the cannons—had broken loose, and the gundeck was now an immense bowling alley, capable of overturning the ship.

Anson battled Cape Horn storms for more than a month, holding his ship west against the wind and the current. Belowdecks, men were dying of scurvy, a foul disease that seemed to kill by melting human flesh. What it actually did was dissolve connective tissue— rotting the gums until teeth fell out, swelling old wounds so that they oozed and spurted anew. All over the body, the skin became ulcerated as blood vessels leaked; death came from burst blood vessels in the brain. With every man needed to run the ship there was nobody to care for the sick, and they died in their hammocks. The bodies were then carried to the main deck, still in their hammocks, but it sometimes happened that there was nobody able to bury them by throwing them overboard. Corpses rolled around on the deck while awaiting burial.

When *Centurion* finally broke free of the Cape—when the navigator's dead reckoning told him they were ten degrees west of the westernmost point of Tierra del Fuego—Anson turned the ship north. They were headed for fresh water and sunshine, and the green islands of Juan Fernández. There the shredded sails and splintered masts could be replaced, the sick carried ashore to be nursed back to health. The Juan Fernández islands, with their waterfalls and grassy meadows and lime trees, were familiar to all book-reading Britons as the setting for Daniel Defoe's *Robinson Crusoe*. Although written as fiction, the novel had its basis in the true adventures of Alexander Selkirk, a Scottish sailor marooned for four years on one of Juan Fernández's three islands.

These life-giving islands lay four hundred miles off the coast of

Chile, their latitude roughly the same as Santiago's. The skies were still clouded over, men were still dying, but there was hope now, for every day brought them closer to Juan Fernández.

Then, in mid-April, on a night of comparative calm, the mist lifted a little toward morning, and what Anson saw through patchy fog amazed and horrified him. There was land dead ahead—only two miles distant. They were sailing north, there should be nothing but empty ocean ahead, and all the same they were almost face-to-face with land looming up, waiting for them as the Scillies had waited for Clowdisley Shovell.

The ship was quickly put about, reversing course, and Anson realized where they were. The land ahead was Tierra del Fuego. Still. Instead of rounding the Horn, they had been locked in place and immobilized, like a swimmer treading water, by the powerful eastward current. They were some two hundred miles off course, and not even Harrison's watch-machine could have helped them, for the charts they used—Edmond Halley's charts—were likewise in error by several hundred miles.

Anson had no choice but to do it again: go south and southwest, break free of the Horn, then head north. And he had to do it before there were so many corpses that the living could no longer manage the sails. He plowed through heavy seas, the deck under water much of the time, the crew eating bread that they toasted over flaming brandy to kill the lice and other vermin. Forty men died from scurvy in April alone, but by the end of the month they were finally west of the Horn.

It was then that Anson made an impulsive decision. He would steer straight for Juan Fernández. Without any sure means of knowing longitude, the usual method for finding such a small place in a vast ocean was to get into its latitude, either a long way east of it or a long way west. Once the latitude was reached, the ship could sail the parallel until she saw her destination.

But *Centurion* was rapidly losing her lifeblood—her sailors—and Anson therefore chose the course that was not safe and sure. By heading straight north, rather than diagonally west or east, he reached the islands' latitude, thirty-three and a half degrees south of the equator. Now he had only to make a short trip either east or west. But which was it? He ran westward, and after several days decided he was wrong. He ran east and then sighted land, but it was the rocky coast of Chile, so he turned back and ran westward over the same track until at long last he came to Juan Fernández. Later, he learned that he had been only hours away from it when he halted his first run to the west.

They had reached safe harbor, a warm sweet smell of tropical vegetation floated out over the water to greet them, but men were still dying. It took three days of rowing back and forth to carry all the sick ashore because there were so few able-bodied men to do the carrying. Anson ordered the officers who were still in good health to share the work, he even pitched in himself, yet twelve men died in the rowboats. More than seventy had died during their six hundred miles of zigzagging through the Pacific as they hunted for Juan Fer-

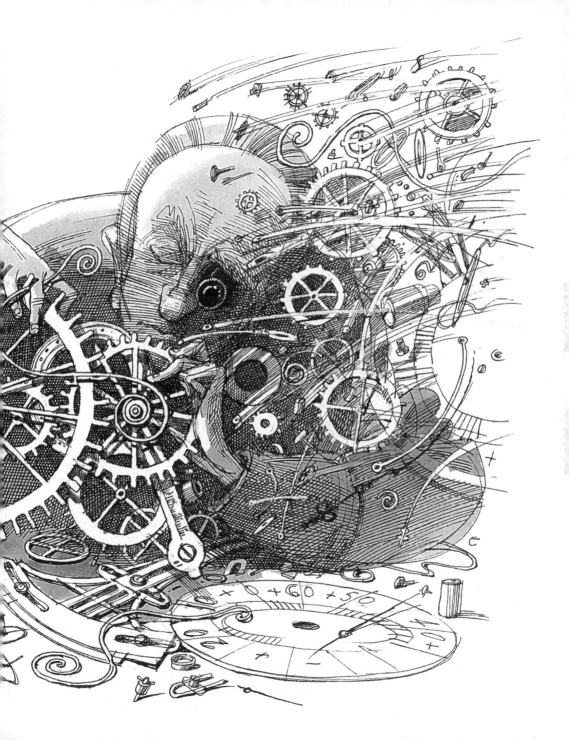

nández and safety. The watch-machine that could have saved them was at home with Harrison in Red Lion Square.

The story of Anson and *Centurion* does not end with Juan Fernández. The ship was repaired; of the six ships in the original squadron only three remained, and all hands were gathered aboard the *Centurion*. They sailed north along the Pacific coast, attacking Spanish ships, capturing and looting the town of Paita, in Peru. The sailors put on the dresses of Spanish ladies and danced by way of celebration.

Heading west, they crossed the Pacific Ocean on the long, dangerous journey to Macao, on the southern coast of China. There they put in for ship repairs and fresh provisions, after which they plied the waters between Macao and the Philippines. They were waiting for a Spanish treasure ship, a galleon that sailed each year from Acapulco, Mexico, to the Philippines.

Centurion met and captured the galleon, *Nuestra Señora de Covadonga*, hauled her back to Macao, and sold her cargo to the Chinese. Anson kept the treasure of solid gold ingots, and gold and silver coin, whose value would come to about fifty million pounds in today's money—no greater prize has been captured by an English ship before or since. Part of the prize money would go to the Admiralty, leaving the rest to be shared by *Centurion*'s officers and sailors, although not equally.

When they returned to England by way of the Cape of Good Hope, at the southern tip of Africa, Anson had circled the globe—

the fourteenth in a line of circumnavigators that began in 1519, with Magellan. In July of 1744, a London newspaper reported: "Yesterday the money taken by Admiral Anson was carried through the city in thirty-two wagons, preceded by a kettle-drum, trumpets, and French horns guarded by the seamen, commanded by the Officers richly dressed, and was lodged in the Tower." The voyage had cost more than a thousand lives. Not one of the Chelsea pensioners survived to come home.

George Anson was now a very rich man, as well as the nation's greatest naval hero. It was understood that he had done his best to save lives; even relatives of the dead sailors acknowledged it. And he had earned the respect of his crew by sharing some of their misfortunes. Appointed to the Admiralty, Anson devoted himself to much-needed reforms of the Royal Navy, and to the conquest of scurvy.

As for John Harrison, while the *Covadonga's* treasure was being paraded in triumph through the streets of London, he was still wrestling with what he called "my curious third machine." According to minutes of the Board of Longitude, he came before them once, during those long years, to say that this clock had "so entirely ingrossed his time & thoughts for many years past as to render him quite incapable of following any gainful employment for the support of himself & family." They granted the funds he asked for, that time as well as others.

This new clock was lighter and more compact than the first two, although one observer said its case resembled "the Body of a Coach and would hold a Child of 4 years old within it." Unlike the earlier clocks, it consisted of about seven hundred different parts and was so designed that to take it apart, make adjustments, and then reassemble it took some eight hours. Harrison must have done this countless times, yet there is no sign that he ever lost heart. On the contrary, he said he had learned so much from H-3 that it was "worth all the money and time it cost," and he fully believed it could be made accurate to within three or four seconds a week.

Among the things he learned was a way of adapting the principle of his gridiron pendulum to the needs of a sea clock, which cannot use a pendulum. Instead of alternating rods of brass and steel, thin strips of the two metals were riveted together into one solid piece, becoming a bimetallic strip that would react immediately and automatically to temperature changes. It was a truly versatile invention; even today, most households use the strip as a thermostatic control—in central heating, in toasters, irons, and electric kettles. Another long-lived invention was the caged roller bearing, an antifriction device that survives today as the caged ball bearing used in almost every machine.

During those lean and difficult years—and while the curious third machine was eating up Harrison's life—the Royal Society made a handsome gesture of support. They had stood by him from the start. Now they awarded him their Copley Gold Medal, the highest honor they were capable of giving; a speech by Martin Folkes, the Society's president, paid tribute to Harrison's modesty and perseverance. Modest he certainly was, for in the flurry of pamphlets and broadsheets he published later he never once mentioned the Copley medal. (Joseph Priestley, who discovered oxygen; Ernest Rutherford, who discovered the structure of the atom; and Albert Einstein, who formulated the theory of relativity, were among subsequent winners.)

Harrison had become a thoroughgoing Londoner by then. Other Londoners knew all about him; they knew what he was doing, and why; they called him "Longitude" Harrison. George Graham borrowed H-1 for a time and displayed it in his shop, and people came from all over to admire it. Pierre Le Roy, a celebrated French clockmaker, called it "a most ingenious contrivance." To the artist William Hogarth it was "one of the most exquisite movements ever made." Even America heard about it, for in 1757, soon after Benjamin Franklin's arrival in London, he made it his business to go to "Harrison's to see his Longitude clock."

And in that same year, 1757, the longitude system based on movements of the moon—the one that Godfrey and Hadley designed their reflecting quadrants for—took a significant step forward, striding to center stage. A young German geographer, Tobias Mayer, had worked out lunar tables that showed the moon's location at twelve-hour intervals. In 1755 he sent them to Anson, now Admiral Lord Anson and chairman of the Board of Longitude. Anson gave them to James Bradley, the Astronomer Royal, who compared them with observations of his own, made at Greenwich, and found them impressive. But their true value could be judged only by extensive testing at sea, and for this purpose Bradley chose a naval officer named John Campbell.

In 1740, at the age of twenty, Campbell had left England aboard HMS *Centurion*, on which he served as Anson's navigator, so he knew firsthand what ignorance of the longitude could cost in human lives. By 1757 Britain was once more at war, this time with France, but Campbell managed to test the new lunar tables on and off for the next two years, aboard HMS *Royal George*, and often within sight of enemy territory. Since a voyage of any great distance was clearly impossible under wartime restrictions, the tests were not considered conclusive—but at the same time, they were wonderfully promising, for they showed an error of less than one degree of longitude. Half a degree was the goal, the Holy Grail that everyone concerned with longitude was aiming at.

It began to seem possible, even likely, that these tables would be the basis of the lunar method Newton and Halley and so many others had believed in and waited for. Like the system for measuring longitude on land, using the comings and goings of Jupiter's moons, the lunar method is built on the idea of the heavens as a clock. The pathway of the moon as it glides across the sky, passing among the fixed stars, is visible from every place on earth. Therefore we imagine the stars as the clock's dial, the moon as the clock's single hand.

If an astronomer in London could work out charts of the moon's

path for months ahead, the charts could then be given to a navigator and taken to sea. Once at sea, on any cloudless night he could watch for the moment when the moon's path touched on any one particular star and compare it with the time that same meeting of moon and star took place in London. He would then work out his longitude by finding the difference in hours between the two places, and multiplying by 15 degrees—since the earth makes a complete 360-degree rotation in twenty-four hours, meaning it turns 15 degrees every hour.

In theory, all of this was possible even when Edmond Halley was young. In practice, there were serious obstacles. In the early eighteenth century there was still no accurate way of predicting the moon's future movements. And there was still no complete map of the heavens; neither were there precision instruments for measuring the altitude of a heavenly body, or its distance from any other heavenly body.

The 1730s brought Hadley's reflecting quadrant; both in England and abroad, astronomers had continued the work of cataloguing stars, sharing their knowledge across national borders. It was the third part of the puzzle—predicting the moon's pathway—that continued to defy the most persistent attack. Newton called it "the only problem that ever made my head ache."

Now the problem showed signs of giving way. John Harrison was surely aware of this; he must have been following reports of Campbell's tests, he certainly knew what they meant, and while there are no clues to his thoughts or feelings on the subject, we know what he did.

In July of 1760 he informed the Board of Longitude that H-3, his third clock, was finished at last. Nineteen years of his life had gone into it.

6

THE FIRST REAL, OFFICIAL SEA TRIAL

hen Harrison appeared before the Board that summer of 1760, supposedly to discuss a sea trial for H-3, he had something else on his mind, something he would keep to himself until midway through the session.

No doubt he wanted to create a stir, to take the meeting by surprise and upset the expectations of its members. If so, he had good reasons for it. The Board of Longitude had changed considerably since their first interview with Harrison, twenty-three years earlier. For that matter, the scientific community as a whole had changed. It seemed to be full of new people now, with new ideas, in a very great hurry to make their mark on the world. Edmond Halley was dead, replaced as Astronomer Royal by James Bradley. Bradley would die soon, his replacement would also die in short order, and the next Astronomer Royal would be one of the new people, a talented young man in a hurry for success. George Graham was dead as well, and Martin Folkes, who had been president of the Royal Society, and made such a graceful speech when awarding Harrison the Copley medal.

The Copley medal was an important honor, but that was long ago, or seemed like long ago. Meanwhile, the Board had invested over two thousand pounds in Harrison's clock, the third one, the one he kept promising to finish; for nineteen years, they had been handing out money without getting anything in return. So it was understandable that they should see him now as an elderly mechanic, ineffectual and unreliable—a remnant of a bygone era.

Nobody pointed out to them that the Harrison family had been living for all that time on a little over a hundred pounds a year, less than half the salary of a lower civil servant. In effect, the government's two thousand pounds had bought nineteen years' worth of first-class scientific research. But the Board didn't see it that way and therefore didn't expect much from Harrison and this clock, which might not be finished even now. Which might not ever be finished.

And when he told the members that H-3 was ready—now—for a trial at sea, they must have been mildly surprised. Moreover, this announcement was followed by another that was even more surprising. He had something to show them, he said. According to the minutes of the meeting, that something proved to be another timekeeper, not large, clumsy, and overweight, but a watch. It was a slim, dazzling beauty of a watch, five inches in diameter, encased in silver, resembling the sort of pocket watch a gentleman might wear if that gentleman happened to be a giant with elegant taste. Inside the outer, protective case lay an inner plate covered with a fantasy of fluting, all of it embellished by exquisite engraving and pierced work. The plate served to cover the innards of the watch, which were lavishly jeweled with rubies and diamonds to guard against friction. Although jeweled bearings were not Harrison's invention, such an extensive use of them was almost revolutionary. At the heart of the watch lay a small balance, beating a rapid five swings each second. This, too, was revolutionary, for the high-frequency oscillator made possible a far more stable timekeeper than the earlier, massive clocks.

A lifetime of self-denial had gone into the silver watch, the labor of two hands that were never idle, the constant searching of an inventive and restless mind that refused to admit defeat. Harrison's feelings about his watch were revealed in a rare moment of eloquence, when he wrote: "I think I may make bold to say, that there is neither any other Mechanism or Mathematical thing in the World that is more beautiful or curious in texture than this my watch or Time-keeper for the Longitude . . . and I heartily thank Almighty

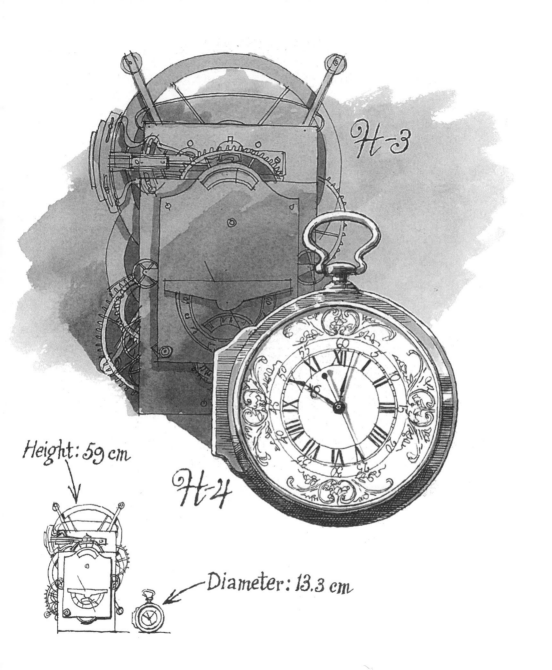

H-3

H-4

Height: 59 cm

Diameter: 13.3 cm

God that I have lived so long, as in some measure to complete it."

The Board members knew Harrison had been working on this watch for the past five years. They might even have seen mechanical drawings for it at an earlier meeting. But to have it actually ticking away before them—slender, compact, exquisite—must have caused a sensation. Surely they wondered how a maker of extremely large clocks had managed to transform himself into a watchmaker; it was an entirely different craft. And why had he done it, when everybody knew that a pocket watch was not a serious timekeeper?

Most of all, they must have wondered what was going on inside the silver case, but they wondered in vain. Years were to pass before Harrison showed its works, and then it was only under considerable pressure. Yet the minutes of the meeting tell us that he spoke of its performance with the greatest confidence. The watch still needed finer adjustment for temperature, he said, and that would have to wait until winter. But by the spring of next year both H-3 and the silver watch would be ready for sea trials. In the meanwhile, as always, he needed something to live on.

The promise of two longitude machines must have been tempting, even for this group of skeptics, for they granted the money, and John Harrison went back to his workshop in Red Lion Square.

What followed was a kind of sleight of hand—a parlor trick, with one object substituted for another while the audience was distracted by harmless patter. This bit of magic was almost certainly motivated by Harrison's anxiety about Tobias Mayer and the new lunar tables.

And what happened was that H-3 faded from view, then disappeared.

Although Harrison told the Board he had perfected it, and "was ready to make a trial of the same when directed to do so," he must have been aware of certain basic flaws in its design. He had tried repeatedly to compensate for these flaws, which involved the balance springs. But he never succeeded.

Then why did he say the clock was finished, and ready to be tried at sea? This was surely done for the sake of H-4, the silver watch. With most of his friends and supporters gone, the time must inevitably come when the Board was no longer willing to hand out money. Without money, work on H-4 would be cut off—there would be no sea trial; watch-machines would drop out of sight and out of history, and their inventor along with them.

This is only speculation, of course, but it is the generally agreed-upon explanation of events. Harrison's "curious third machine" was put aside, as the silver watch, which was to become the most famous timekeeper ever made, took its place.

An engraving on its back plate tells us it was built by John Harrison and Son, the son being William, who was then in his early thirties and had been working for years as his father's right-hand man. Like his uncle James before him, William was no great lover of clocks, although he knew a good deal about them. But he was devoted to his father and his father's interests—which were also his interests, since he would inherit the famous prize if it could be won—and he was enterprising, dependable, with strong family loyalties.

In February of the following year, a letter from John Harrison told the Board that the silver watch was performing with amazing accuracy. He was ready for an official trial at sea, he said, and the members agreed to it. Yet it seems they were unprepared for this request, even though they must have known it was coming.

According to Harrison's biographer, Humphrey Quill, it's hard to believe that the Board members "regarded the projected trial with any great seriousness. It seems possible that they viewed the test merely as a means by which it could be ascertained whether or not a portable timekeeper could *ever* be expected to provide a practical way of finding the longitude at sea." As a result, they gave him only a few verbal instructions, which were in any case incomplete and unclear.

Since John Harrison was now sixty-seven, too old for an ocean voyage, it was agreed that William should take charge of the timekeeper on this possible sea trial to the West Indies. He was told to go to Portsmouth, outfit himself for the voyage, and await further orders; his father would follow with the watch.

So William left his pregnant wife at home in London and went to Portsmouth, where he stayed in the home of a friend. To pass the time, he planted a row of beans in his friend's garden, knowing he could hardly expect to see them grow. Meanwhile, his wife gave birth to a son they called John, after his grandfather, and the beans grew until they were ready to harvest, and five months later William was still waiting. In October, furious about the wasted time, he gave up and went home.

His father had used the five months to fine-tune the silver watch, but he, too, had every reason to resent this casual, offhand, even insulting treatment.

Then, in November, William was told to return to Portsmouth, where he would board HMS *Deptford* and sail for Jamaica. Events moved briskly now. In spite of the unfortunate beginning, this time the sea trial was real and official—the first official test of a Harrison watch-machine, as well as the first official six-weeks-to-the-Indies trial of any longitude system.

Rules and procedures for the trial were laid out with help from the Royal Society: before sailing, local time in Portsmouth must be calculated in the usual way, by finding local noon—the moment when the sun is at its highest. This was done with a specialized telescope called an "equal-altitude instrument," and to do it properly, observations had to be taken several times, some well before noon, some well after. It goes without saying that equal-altitude observations could not be made in bad weather.

The same procedure was to take place at journey's end, in Jamaica, where John Robison, an astronomer assigned to sail aboard the *Deptford*, was to find exact local noon by equal altitudes of the sun. If the watch had kept perfect time throughout the voyage, the difference between noon in Portsmouth and noon in Jamaica would be precisely the same as the difference between Jamaica's known longitude and the known longitude of Portsmouth. And if it had kept less than perfect time, the amount of disagreement would be the error of the watch during the voyage.

Another condition set by the Royal Society: the watch must be kept in a box, this box to have four locks. Four people would hold one key apiece: William, Captain Dudley Digges, his first lieutenant, and the governor of Jamaica, a passenger. All four must be present whenever the box was opened. Because John Harrison had lost faith in gimbals, the watch was to rest between two soft cushions in its box, and William would have to adjust its position frequently in order to keep it level.

In Portsmouth, as they made ready to sail in the autumn of 1761, the skies were often partly clouded, and although equal altitudes were taken on four different days by the Board's appointed astronomer, there was a general feeling that they were starting out under a handicap. There was another difficulty, one that would be apparent only later on, that had to do with something called rate.

Any watch can be expected to lose or gain in a twenty-four-hour period; this is true even of modern watches. And if the loss or gain is by the same amount each day—if the watch has a steady rate—the right time can always be calculated. If the loss or gain is irregular, it then becomes impossible to work out the right time. The trouble here was that the Harrisons expected to apply a rate to the readings of the silver watch, a perfectly reasonable expectation if they had said so in advance. It seems they did not.

William and the watch set off for Jamaica in November of 1761, and for the next five years we will see the Harrisons somewhat more clearly than we have before. This is because of a private journal that was kept for them by a friend. The journal may have been written out from notes jotted down by either John or William, but the handwriting—it has never been printed—belongs to neither one. The style is usually impersonal, which is unfortunate. Nevertheless, there are passages here and there that bring John Harrison to life before our eyes, touchy and easily angered, likely to say whatever comes into his head. The journal writer, on the other hand, is a pompous person—like William—and the manuscript is usually referred to as "William's journal."

The first event of interest is the transatlantic crossing itself. A square-rigged ship of the *Deptford*'s type usually went south to the islands of Madeira, to pick up trade winds that would blow it steadily southwest toward the West Indies, and this was the course the ship took. After ten days at sea the crew hoped to sight the Madeiras.

When they were nine days out, it was discovered that more than a thousand gallons of beer had spoiled, and there was no choice but to throw it overboard. Before long the rest of the beer supply followed. Since sailing ships had no way of storing fresh water, this was a serious loss, for it left the crew with nothing to drink but bilge-water from the hold, a vile and stinking soup in which vermin flourished.

The sailors comforted themselves with talk of Madeira and its famous wines. At the same time, they knew it was also possible to miss the Madeiras, to sail for days, sometimes weeks, in search of them, without any sure way of finding longitude, such delays were commonplace. But days or weeks of water shortage would endanger the health of the crew as well as its morale, and everyone aboard was anxious for a landfall.

After ten days at sea the captain began to wonder about their position. They were in the right latitude for Madeira, but he was unsure whether it lay to the west or the east, or how far. Turning to William, he asked what Mr. Harrison thought.

William claimed they were exactly on course for Porto Santo, one of the Madeira Islands, and if they kept to their course they would see it tomorrow morning. According to the watch-machine, he added, their longitude was almost one hundred miles farther west than the position given by the navigator's dead reckoning.

Captain Digges, who thought this was nonsense, offered odds of five to one that William was wrong. But the purpose of the voyage was to test the watch-machine, so he told the navigator to hold his course. By seven the next morning they saw the Madeiras.

The captain then begged to be allowed to buy the first longitude watch that the Harrisons built for sale to the public. And he wrote a letter to John Harrison, to be enclosed with one William was writing at the time, in which he described "the great perfection of your watch." When they left Porto Santo for Jamaica, William must have been delighted with the sturdy performance of H-4—its performance so far, that is.

For the first ten days were only one leg of their transatlantic voyage, and everything depended on what they found when they came to Jamaica. If the watch fell short, then all was lost. William knew his father was too old to correct its faults, too old to construct another and better timekeeper. And the margin for error was so very small—three seconds a day during a voyage of several thousand miles, aboard a small, unstable ship.

On January 19, 1762, after two months at sea, they reached Port Royal, Jamaica. No sooner had William and John Robison, the astronomer, set foot on land than difficulties sprang up on every side. Because the weather was cloudy, they had trouble taking the equal altitudes that would fix local time; on one day they managed to do it, but the next day was cloudy again. They were told by the island's governor that no homebound ship would sail for another six months, so they assumed there would be plenty of time for equal altitudes, but on January 25 William learned that war had just been declared with Spain. A ship would be leaving for England on the twenty-eighth. The governor told him to be on it.

In the rush of departure, William and Robison agreed that if they accepted the known longitude of Jamaica—the one shown on maps and charts—then the total error of the silver watch amounted to all of five seconds. It was a triumphant, even an incredible performance. If William had any doubts about it, those doubts would have risen from the equal-altitude readings. There should have been more readings, and he knew it, but the weather and the premature sailing were beyond his control.

On the homeward journey, aboard a little sloop called Merlin, a furious storm overtook them in mid-Atlantic. William described it in a letter to a relative: "We had the most Turbolent voyage home that was possible . . . it was the greatest marvel in the World that it [the watch] kept going at all, for I plas'd it in the Cabbin quite astarne upon the seat or counter, and when we lay-to . . . it received such shocks from the breaking of the waves under the Counter, that it was just as if I had taken the box in my hand and thrown it from one side of the Cabbin to the other."

The decks were under two feet of water; even the captain's cabin was six inches deep at times. Once the rudder broke in a very hard gale, "but it pleas'd God to send us 3 or 4 hours moderate weather to mend it again, and then came on the heaviest wind that ever man on board had seen blow. We had nothing to look at or Expect but every wave that came would send us to the Bottom."

Although horribly seasick, William devoted himself to keeping the watch box dry. He was determined at all costs to make sure the watch never stopped going, for fear people might claim it was too delicate to survive at sea, so he covered the box with a blanket. Whenever the blanket had soaked up as much water as he could squeeze out with one hand, he found another blanket. To make sure there was always a dry one, he wrapped himself in several wet, cold blankets when he went to sleep, hoping his body heat would dry them out, and this combined with the seasickness threw him "into a severe fit of illness."

When he reached England on a cloudy day in March 1762, he was still sick. But it hardly mattered now, because he was able to give his father the glorious news. John Harrison heard for the first time that all of five seconds were lost on the two-month voyage to Jamaica. Five seconds, when adjusted for rate, according to findings made by Robison and William upon landing at Port Royal. It was almost unbelievable, almost too good to be true, and yet it was true. After a lifetime of labor, John Harrison had conquered the longitude in an official test, under official conditions, with an officially appointed astronomer doing the calculations.

The Board of Longitude heard about it. The Royal Society heard. There was a new King on the British throne, George III, a tall, pleasant-looking young man who collected scientific instruments. He, too, heard, and wanted to know more about the inventor of such an astounding device.

But clouds had greeted William when he got off the ship, shaking with fever, and before long it began to seem that the calculations made so properly and officially in Jamaica were also clouded over. The long and painful conflict between the moon and the watch-machine was about to begin.

7

FURTHER TRIALS OF JOHN HARRISON AND HIS WATCH

n January of 1761, almost a year before William and the watch sailed for Jamaica, another ship left England for the remote South Atlantic island of St. Helena. It carried a young man assigned by the Royal Society to set up an astronomical observatory there. His name was Nevil Maskelyne, and he enters these pages for the first but not the last time.

He had many friends in the Royal Society, although he was not yet a member. He had influential friends in several places, one of them being his brother-in-law, Robert Clive, known as Clive of

India for having defeated the Nawab of Bengal in 1757 at the Battle of Plassey, which won for Britain its foothold in India and the beginnings of empire. Maskelyne had an especially important ally and friend in James Bradley, the Astronomer Royal, whom he met soon after leaving Cambridge.

What Nevil Maskelyne wanted more than anything in life was to become a great astronomer himself, if possible an Astronomer Royal. With this in mind, he had wangled the assignment to St. Helena, where Edmond Halley had gone almost a century earlier. And during the three-month voyage he planned to continue what Captain John Campbell began: the testing of Mayer's lunar tables.

His instruments included a Hadley's quadrant, one of a new type, specially designed for lunar-distance measurements. He carried two reflecting telescopes made by James Short, an astronomer and instrument maker who was a supporter of John Harrison. And among his personal supplies were three gallons of lemon juice to guard against scurvy—in this Maskelyne was far ahead of his time—as well as a generous store of wines and liquor, to be shared with his manservant.

In his first report to the Royal Society, Maskelyne told them he had made at least sixteen lunar-distance observations, and that upon arrival in St. Helena his longitude error was less than one degree—while the ship's officers, using dead reckoning, had errors of up to ten degrees. With Mayer's tables and one of the new quadrants, he said, anyone with enough "leisure and ability to make the requisite calculations will be able to ascertain his Longitude . . . as near as will be in general required."

The word "leisure" is important here. Nevil Maskelyne, a trained mathematician and astronomer, needed four hours of intense concentration to calculate longitude with Mayer's tables. But he was thoroughly convinced of their usefulness and practicality, so much so that on the homeward voyage he encouraged the ship's officers to take observations themselves, and he showed them how to do the calculations. Seamen called this process "doing lunars."

In March of 1762, when William reached England after the Jamaica trial of the silver watch, Maskelyne was still at sea, headed for home aboard an East Indiaman. He arrived in May, and a month later an account of his successful use of Mayer's tables was read to the Royal Society.

They were thoroughly delighted with Mayer and with Maskelyne; so was the Board of Longitude. The four hours were not important to them, even though a ship without an accurate longitude reading can go down in four minutes. What was important about Mayer-and-Maskelyne was that it helped to justify the Board's deep-rooted faith in lunars. As a further expression of faith, they gave him permission to publish a handbook on the subject, one that would serve as a complete guide to the use of lunars. It was to be made available to all seagoing men.

John Harrison, of course, saw matters differently. He knew that recent developments in the lunar system were a serious threat to the success of his watch-machine. And for some time he had suspected the Board of favoring lunars. These suspicions are clearly expressed in what he wrote during the years ahead, and what William wrote. Sometimes they seem overly suspicious, almost fantastically so; but generally speaking, it was quite true that the odds were against him, and that in the eyes of many on the Board of Longitude lunars deserved to win.

There were several reasons for it. To begin with, the lunar system had a distinguished ancestry. The basic principles were known as early as the sixteenth century, described by Johann Werner of Nuremberg in 1514. And Werner was thought to be indebted to the great fifteenth-century astronomer and mathematician Regiomontanus, who proposed using lunar eclipses to work out the longitude of places on land. Even this was not new, since the use of lunar eclipses for longitude had been mentioned by Ptolemy, in the second century A.D., and earlier by Hipparchus, c. 180–125 B.C.

To members of the Board—whose education had included generous doses of Latin and ancient history, along with a deep respect for the classics—the lunar system had credentials, the watch-machine had none. Also, the position of Astronomer Royal, usually the most powerful member of the Board, had been created with lunars in mind—for he was supposed to rectify "the Tables of the Motions of the Heavens, and the Places of the fixed Stars," in order to find longitude at sea.

The Board members believed in lunars for another and more poetic reason. There was something noble about the system, an almost religious quality, since it concerned the moon, the stars, the eternal heavens; it lifted human eyes upward toward the firmament. They knew little about clocks or clockmaking, but they knew that ordinary watches were highly unreliable. And that even a silver watch was only a ticking mechanism, not noble, not eternal, created not by the hand of God but by mortal and imperfect hands.

Finally, there were the words of Isaac Newton: "And I have told you oftener then once that it [the longitude at sea] is not to be found by Clock-work . . . Nothing but Astronomy is sufficient for this purpose. But if you are unwilling to meddle with Astronomy . . . I am unwilling to meddle with any other methods."

And when all was said and done, there were reasons that had nothing to do with reason, but with the mystery of personality—Harrison's personality. When he first appeared before the gentlemen of the Board, in 1737, they had listened with interest. When he showed them his sea clock they had high hopes for it, even though many of them were already committed to a lunar solution. As for Harrison himself, they accepted him as readily as Edmond Halley had. Maybe they never noticed the roughness of manner, the tactlessness that Halley saw from the start—but if they did, they knew it didn't matter. The work mattered, and his was brilliantly original.

By 1762, with most of his old friends gone—with H-1 a distant memory, and nothing substantial to show for all the succeeding years—there was a different climate. Because the Board members

The Board believed in lunars.

now were lukewarm about sea clocks and enthusiastic about lunars, their reactions to him were colored accordingly. Sometimes they were indifferent, sometimes discourteous. This had the unlucky effect of putting Harrison's back up.

The years directly ahead would bring out his least attractive traits: his temper, impatience, and rudeness. The Board might have overlooked such behavior from a gentleman; not all of those who were well born were well mannered. But a gentleman was likely to learn early on what he could get away with. When someone had the upper hand, whether by birth or position, it was best to tiptoe around—at least until the wind shifted, after which that someone would do the tiptoeing. The important thing was knowing when and how, something Harrison never learned.

We hear about it in various ways, sometimes from minutes of the Board, sometimes, although less often, by reading between the lines of William's journal—how his father flew off the handle, stomped out of meetings, turned his back on an Astronomer Royal. And the Board could not accept such behavior as that earlier Board had, in Halley's time—knowing the work mattered, not the man. The man did matter to this Board, and Harrison was the wrong kind of man.

For one thing, he had the wrong accent. In England, speech was the most telling clue to a man's background and station in life. A Yorkshireman had a certain speech pattern, the man from Cumberland had another, as did the London-bred Cockney, and so forth. An entirely different speech pattern, almost another language, belonged to the gentry. It had nothing to do with where they were born. It was simply the King's English, or "proper" English, or at any rate the opposite of "common" English. And of course it was the speech pattern of all members of the Board, their friends, wives, children, and the governesses entrusted with bringing up those children. Governesses who spoke proper English.

Every time Harrison opened his mouth they heard the accent that marked him as common—a hayseed, an oaf, an unschooled villager from some North Country place or other. And he had yet another drawback in William, who was not his father's best ally before the Board.

According to Jonathan Betts, Curator of Horology at the National Maritime Museum, William comes across in contemporary accounts "as a decidedly objectionable character"—a bootlicker and toady "of a most unpleasant kind." It seems unjust that someone as downright as John Harrison, without a shred of hypocrisy or snobbishness in him, should have had such a son. But he did. And whenever the elder Harrison came before the Board, William, like the accent, came with him.

How significant were these personal matters in the conflict between the moon and the watch-machine? It's not easy to know. Harrison's character was certainly not the primary cause of his problems. If Bradley had not died so soon, or if Nathaniel Bliss, his successor as Astronomer Royal, who died after only two years in that post, had been followed by someone more sympathetic to Harrison, the chain of events might have been different—he might have held on to his temper, his accent might have been considered picturesque. As it was, his not being a gentleman was surely a serious irritant in an already inflamed situation.

At this point in the narrative the Harrisons had been waiting for the next meeting of the Board, the one that would react to the Jamaica sea trial. Days and weeks went by; the weeks became months. Then a meeting was announced for the third of June, and both Harrisons went to it. If they hoped for praise, recognition, an end to the years of unrewarded labor, surely they had a right to do so.

But according to William's journal, "great fault" was found with his observations. Robison, the astronomer, was closely questioned by the Board, especially about the instruments he used. Much was said about the longitude of Jamaica, with the Board demanding to know why the expedition failed to take a new longitude reading based on Jupiter's moons, although there were no instructions for doing this, as the Board most certainly knew.

Worst of all, they refused to accept the claim that H-4 lost only five seconds on the outward-bound voyage. This result was based on a rate, and the Harrisons had failed to declare a rate before sailing. The Board concluded that three mathematicians must be set to work, checking the calculations and the instruments for errors.

At a later meeting there were fresh attacks on Harrison. This time the Board members pointed out that they knew nothing about the mechanism of the silver watch, since John Harrison had never let them see it. Therefore it was quite possible that its performance on the voyage to Jamaica was a fluke. Would it do so well a second time? Suppose some adventurer took twelve dozen watches to Jamaica, they said; surely one of them could have shown the right time entirely by accident.

Everywhere the Harrisons looked, they saw doubt, confusion, disapproval. When the three mathematicians turned in their report, it was said to be unfavorable. Perhaps it was, but perhaps it was so favorable that the Board found themselves unable to believe it. In any case, the report was never made public, and never will be, since it has unaccountably disappeared.

The Board's final verdict about the Jamaica trial went as follows: "that the Experiments already made of the Watch have not been sufficient to determine the Longitude at Sea." All the same, they admitted that the watch was "an invention of considerable utility to the Public," and awarded Harrison 2,500 pounds, of which 1,500 pounds would be paid immediately, the rest to follow when the watch returned from a fresh trial to the Indies.

It seems John Harrison had done the impossible: created a timekeeper of which he was tremendously proud, which told the longitude better than even he had hoped. And instead of recognition he was repaid with doubt, with checkings and testings and mathematicians.

He agreed to this second trial, "if it will end all disputes," as the journal notes—but it was at this point that his respect for the Board became suspicion. He saw plots, maneuverings, prejudice. Sometimes they were imaginary, sometimes real.

As for the Board, they were never dishonest in their dealings with him, and they never did anything illegal. But they were not going to hand over 20,000 pounds of the nation's money to this clockmaker without resisting every inch of the way, and their judgment about the first sea trial was only the opening salvo in a battle that would last more than ten years.

Harrison responded with a pamphlet, published anonymously, aimed at Parliament and the public at large: *An Account of the Proceedings in order to the Discovery of the Longitude*. Since the style is concise and clear, the author was obviously not Harrison, and it is generally believed that his friend James Short did the writing of this and other pamphlets. *An Account* gives a straightforward summary of Harrison's work and was intended to stir up popular support.

At the same time, members of the Board, along with some of his allies, began encouraging him to reveal the workings of the silver watch. This Harrison outright refused to do, and with good reason. It would mean taking the watch apart in the presence of witnesses, a time-consuming process. He would then have to reassemble, test, and adjust it, yet the watch had to be ready for its second trial. He wanted to get on with that second trial. He was past seventy now and he had no way of knowing how many years were left to him.

Nevil Maskelyne, on the other hand, was young and ambitious. Thanks to a brief autobiography he wrote in his sixties, it is possible to get some sense of his character. We learn, for example, that he tended to take himself rather seriously. In the opening sentence he tells us that "Dr. M. is the last male heir of an ancient family." "Dr. M." is Nevil Maskelyne, since he chose to write his life's story in the third person—the "doctor" comes from his being a country parson, a way of earning a modest income without much effort.

He then goes on to explain that it was not a rich family, and that when the father died, the son had to make his own way at Cambridge. He went as a sizar, a student who paid reduced fees in exchange for menial work, probably waiting on table. He was never afraid of hard work, was conscientious, something of a plodder, and took very good care of his employees and himself.

And in his own way, as he is revealed in the autobiography, he enjoyed life. His account books kept track of every penny he got or spent for thirty-seven years, but at the same time he was also jotting down jokes, anecdotes, recipes, what wines were served at dinner, and who sat down to drink them.

In 1763, at the age of thirty-one, this conscientious and stuffy gentleman published the book authorized earlier by the Board of Longitude: *The British MARINER'S GUIDE containing Complete and Easy Instructions for the Discovery of the LONGITUDE at Sea and Land, within a Degree, by Observations of the Distance of the Moon from the Sun and Stars, taken with HADLEY'S Quadrant.* Although the process still took four hours, the book was an immediate success. It developed later into *The Nautical Almanac*, published from 1767 until the early years of the twentieth century.

The Harrisons, meanwhile, were waiting for the second trial of the silver watch. Everything connected with it took shape slowly, reluctantly, with much fruitless discussion back and forth between the Harrisons and the Board. They learned that two astronomers were to be sent to Jamaica well in advance of William and the silver watch, that they would build a small observatory there and use it to find the island's longitude by means of Jupiter's moons. And that one of the two chosen astronomers was Nevil Maskelyne.

They learned something else: that the expedition would not go to Jamaica after all but to Barbados—because Nevil Maskelyne had requested the change. Jamaica, he said, was a fever-ridden place.

Apparently there was to be no escape from lunars and Maskelyne. Sometimes the enemy had another name, for instance the Earl of Morton, president of the Royal Society, or Nathaniel Bliss, Bradley's successor as Astronomer Royal. But most often it was Nevil Maskelyne, who was everything Harrison was not: young, well educated, the descendant of an "ancient family," with a gentleman's interest in wine, food, and good company. Harrison never concealed his dislike of the man.

In one of the almost unreadable pamphlets he wrote some years later, this passage appears: ". . . if it please Almighty God, to continue my life and health a little longer, they the Professors (or Priests) shall not hinder me of my pleasure, as from my last drawing, viz. of bringing my watch to a second in a fortnight, I say I am resolved of this, though quite unsuitable to the usage I have had, or was ever to expect from them; and when as Dr. Bradley once said to me (not but what I understood the same without his saying it) viz. that if timekeeping could be to 10 seconds in a week, it would, as with respect to the longitude, be much preferable to any other way or method. And so, as I do not now mind the money (as not having occasion so to do, and withal as being weary of that) the Devil may take the Priests."

By "Professors (or Priests)" he means Nevil Maskelyne, a priest of the Church of England, along with the three university professors appointed to the Board. In other writings, Harrison refers to his enemies as "men of theory"—talkers, not doers, who never built anything, never got their hands dirty; the Devil was welcome to them.

The Reverend Dr. Maskelyne left for Barbados in July of 1763, taking with him a set of greatly improved lunar tables. Tobias Mayer had died the previous year, unexpectedly, at the age of thirty-nine, and before his death he told his wife to send these new tables to the Board, who gave them to Maskelyne, with instructions to try them on the outward voyage. The results were astonishing.

As Maskelyne wrote to his brother, upon sailing into port he was able to predict the ship's position to within half a degree of longitude. Half a degree was almost pinpoint precision.

If such results could be relied on, the system that produced them would qualify for the longitude prize, although Maskelyne said nothing about the prize in his letter home. Meanwhile there was work to be done ashore, and he tackled that next; he supervised the building of the small observatory, and took observations there. His free time was passed agreeably, the letter continues, "to which the great civilities I had received from the gentlemen of this place have not a little contributed."

What, exactly, he said to those gentlemen about longitude and lunars is an interesting question.

William was still in Portsmouth, where he declared the rate of the silver watch would amount to the gaining of one second per day for the length of the voyage. It was March of 1764 before he, too, sailed for Barbados, aboard HMS *Tartar*.

According to his journal, on the day he arrived he went ashore with the watch to find Maskelyne and his assistant, Charles Green—they would record the difference in time between the moment of local noon and the time shown on the watch at the same instant. But in the course of his first day in Barbados, William learned something that shocked him. It seemed Maskelyne had been talking to the local people about lunars and longitude—letting it be known that he, Maskelyne, was excited about the lunar system, and that it was bound to be recognized as the best and surest method for finding longitude at sea. Apparently William also learned—or guessed—that Maskelyne claimed to be a competitor for the great prize.

William reported this to Sir John Lindsay, captain of the *Tartar*. And on Monday morning, so the journal tells us, William and Lindsay together stormed into the observatory at Bridgetown. There William confronted Maskelyne, calling him "a most improper person" to make the observations on which the winning of the prize depended—and gave it as his opinion that the Reverend Dr. Maskelyne could not be trusted.

Maskelyne, who was naturally upset about this slur on his character, insisted on his right to make the observations. Perhaps Sir John acted as arbitrator in this dispute, or perhaps William and Maskelyne battled it out between themselves. One way or another, a compromise was reached: Maskelyne could continue making observations, but must share them half-and-half with the astronomer Charles Green. When Maskelyne went back to his instruments, the journal claims, he was so nervous and angry that he botched his observations.

The episode is puzzling. As John Harrison's biographer, Humphrey Quill, points out, there is no mention of it either in Maskelyne's notes or in the logbook of Captain Lindsay. So we don't know what happened, only that something happened.

Another puzzling aspect: some months after William's return from Barbados, John Harrison was invited to join the Royal Society. It was a distinguished honor; he would be able to write the initials F.R.S.—Fellow of the Royal Society—after his name, and he would attend meetings with the foremost scientific men of the day. But honors held no attraction whatever for Harrison. And it's not easy to picture him eating fried fish and drinking beer at the coffeehouse-tavern in Dean's Court where many of the members gathered before their meetings. So he declined, we hope with grateful thanks.

William was invited to join, at a later date and clearly as a tribute to his father; and since William had no objection to honors, he became an F.R.S. Nevil Maskelyne was one of those who recommended him, the same Nevil Maskelyne whom William accused of being a traitorous competitor, the man whose nervousness and embarrassment that morning were supposed to be sure signs of guilt.

We are left to wonder how much of the story about Maskelyne's boasting to the locals was true, how much was exaggeration. Certainly he believed in lunars; he was an astronomer, and very open about his belief in lunars. But did he truly say he expected to win the prize? There is no evidence that he did, apart from William's report, and he never put in any claim for it, either whole or in part.

As Humphrey Quill observes, "The objections raised by William Harrison reveal the spirit of suspicion and antagonism against Maskelyne that seems to have been continually in his mind, an attitude which was shared by his father."

As for the silver watch, the beating heart of all this dissension, its fate was not yet known. The longitude of Barbados still had to be determined anew, as agreed on before they sailed. This would be done by Maskelyne with the help of his assistant, based on observations of Jupiter's first moon, the one called Io. When William and the watch sailed for home, Maskelyne was still hard at work in the new observatory.

William reached England in midsummer 1764, his spirits soaring because the watch had behaved magnificently on the homeward voyage. And when Nathaniel Bliss, the Astronomer Royal, died two months later, William's optimism increased—"they have now lost their ringleader," he said, of the pro-lunar members of the Board. The promised payment of a thousand pounds, to be given after the second trial of the silver watch, was duly made. Four experts were chosen to do the calculations that would determine its performance on this second trial. And William thanked God for what seemed like a speedy end to his father's difficulties, apparently untroubled by the knowledge that one candidate for the post of Astronomer Royal was Nevil Maskelyne.

The story of Harrison and the longitude prize had been followed in the press for some time now, partly because of Harrison's pamphlets and the strength of the emotions they showed. The selection of a new Astronomer Royal was of interest for the same reason—whoever got the post, that person was sure to play an important role in the ongoing drama of longitude.

James Short, who was Harrison's supporter and unofficial ghostwriter, was one of the prime choices. But the president of the Royal Society, the Earl of Morton, had taken a dislike to Short, "and gives it as a reason that he is a Scotch Man, though he acknowledges that he is the fittest for it of any man"—this cryptic comment is found in a letter sent by an English correspondent to Benjamin Franklin. It was generally agreed that the Earl of Morton disliked Short for no better reason than his being Harrison's friend.

In December of 1764, *The Gentleman's Magazine* published a long poem describing three of the candidates in humorous terms, while praising the fourth, John Bevis, seventy-one years old, a friend of Newton's and Halley's. As for Nevil Maskelyne, "Who . . . skips and prances," he is called a "scientific harlequin," a phrase that might have been used because it rhymed with his second name. The author then reminds his readers that the decision will ultimately be made by Jove, meaning the King. This was not the whole story, since the King leaned heavily on his scientific advisers, and one of the most influential was that same Earl of Morton who had taken a dislike to Short. But the writer never expected Maskelyne to win; neither did the Harrisons.

Some months passed. When the Board of Longitude met in January of 1765, the Harrisons were not invited, although the most important item of business was supposed to be expert testimony about the watch. This testimony was bound to be favorable, as the Harrisons already knew, probably by way of James Short. But before the meeting heard anything about the watch an astonishing piece of news was put before them. A bombshell. The Board announced the appointment of Nevil Maskelyne to the post of Astronomer Royal.

Four experts then delivered their testimony about the silver watch. When adjusted for rate, its average error on the Barbados voyage was slightly more than thirty-nine seconds. According to the terms of the prize, it had performed with triple the accuracy needed for the full sum of 20,000 pounds.

Next, a memorandum from John Harrison was presented, in which he "humbly prayed" for the Board's authority in claiming his prize. The Board thought it over, agreed it was not a thing to be decided quickly, since several members were absent from that particular meeting, and then adjourned for the next three weeks.

Reports of these events—the new Astronomer Royal, the expert testimony, the memorandum that could not be voted on—reached Red Lion Square. We can readily imagine John Harrison's reaction, the mixture of black gloom and triumph, and the suspicion that fate was against him. Why else had Nevil Maskelyne been chosen—why, why, why had James Short been passed over?

On Saturday, the ninth of February, fifteen members came to an all-important meeting of the Board of Longitude, Maskelyne among them, and the Harrisons in attendance. John's memorandum was read again. According to the minutes, members were "unanimously of the opinion that the timekeeper had kept its time with sufficient correctness, and . . . beyond the nearest limit required" for the prize.

But—there was sure to be a but; in all of John Harrison's recent dealings with the Board his successes had bristled with buts—it was explained that according to the rules governing the prize, any method for fixing longitude at sea must first be found "Practicable and Useful."

The Board chose to interpret those words in such a way as to bring John Harrison to his knees. They wanted to see and understand the workings of the silver watch, they said; until they did, they would be unable to judge if it was practical, useful at sea, capable of being copied by others. For a single watch, no matter how marvelous, was no use to the many hundreds of ships that needed guides to the longitude, unless and until it could be duplicated.

It was their duty, therefore, to make sure that other workmen could construct other watch-machines according to Harrison's principles—and that those watch-machines could be produced at a reasonable cost and perform equally well.

With these words ringing in his ears, Harrison heard the next order of business, the reading of a memorandum by His Majesty's new Astronomer Royal, Nevil Maskelyne, in praise of lunars. Four officers of the East India Company then testified that each of them, independently, had followed instructions in Maskelyne's *British Mariner's Guide,* and consistently found their longitude to within one degree. The only difficulty was the calculations, which had taken Maskelyne himself up to four hours to complete.

Maskelyne spoke up next. The solution, he said, was for the Board to begin annual publication of a nautical almanac, based on Mayer's last tables, and containing predictions of lunar distances computed in advance, which would shorten the calculation time. He would be glad to take on responsibility for this almanac, provided the Board was willing to cover the printing fees, and the salaries of two mathematicians.

The Board agreed. Maskelyne then set to work in his usual conscientious way. He decided that all the important calculations would be done by two human "computers," each working at home and on his own. They would send their results to Maskelyne, and he would forward them to a "comparer," so that one man's work could be checked against the other's.

The preparation of this first *Nautical Almanac* was a slow and painstaking business. But almost from the day of publication, in January of 1767, it was a huge success with navigators everywhere. Because of this success—and because Maskelyne calculated all the lunar distances listed in the *Almanac* from the meridian of Greenwich, where he lived and worked—seamen began to do the same; they, too, calculated their longitude from Greenwich. Eventually, the Greenwich meridian was accepted as the prime meridian of the world, the standard for both longitude and time. And this entire chain of events was set in motion by the Board of Longitude's meeting on February 9, 1765, when Nevil Maskelyne first took his place as Astronomer Royal, and John Harrison first learned that a single watch was not enough.

It's important to point out here that there was something to be said both for and against each of the rival methods. If the prize was meant to reward a practical device for longitude at sea, then the watch-machine was not practical, at least not yet. It was much too expensive for ordinary use. Unless English ships could be provided with cheaper watches, they were no better off than before John Harrison set to work in 1730.

Lunars cost very little; nautical instruments had to be bought, along with the standard handbook of navigation, but few captains of the Royal Navy were likely to be put off by the expense. And in

The race for the prize

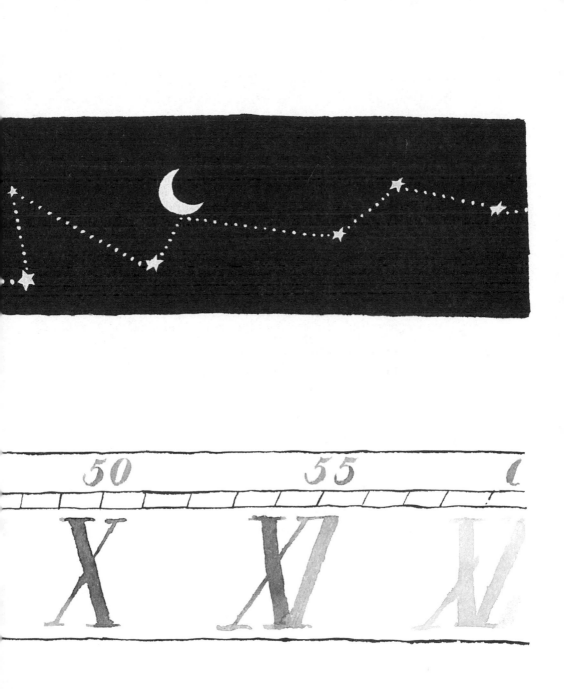

1767, thanks to Maskelyne's *Almanac*, the number of arithmetical calculations required to do lunars was greatly reduced by the use of prefigured tables. Instead of four hours, it was now a matter of thirty minutes—thirty minutes under clear skies.

The method still required a firm grounding in mathematics and astronomy, and there were many who never got that grounding. There were also old salts so tradition-bound that they never wanted it. Besides, when battling a stormy sea, with all hands needed to keep the ship above water, nobody could spare even half an hour. Still, the lunar method might one day be simplified further, made both easier and more reliable. Of course, it was equally true that, in the future, watch-machines might be manufactured cheaply and fast.

The strongest argument on Harrison's side was not the silver watch at all but the principle it proved, that an accurate timekeeper could fix the longitude. If the Board had been able to see into the future, they would have known this and rewarded him on the spot. But they couldn't see into the future any more than Harrison could, so they fought for what seemed to be modern and scientific, for what presented an intellectual challenge worthy of the finest minds, minds like their own. They fought for lunars.

For Nevil Maskelyne, that February meeting was only one in a long successsion of triumphs. And for Harrison, whose watch had won unanimous approval from its judges, there was only bitterness. Unspoken, yet inescapable, was the accusation that he had pulled off an illusion, a fluke, an affair of smoke and mirrors that could not be produced a second time. "But still, they say a watch is but or can but be a watch and that . . . the performance of mine (though nearly to truth itself) must be altogether a deception." He had written these mournful words two years earlier, in response to the same unspoken accusation.

He turned once again to the public at large, firing off fresh pamphlets and broadsheets. He presented a petition to Parliament, listing the basic facts of his claim to the prize, and asking the House of Commons to take his case into consideration and give him "such relief as they shall think meet."

The Board members were still intent on bringing Harrison to heel, and they, too, turned to Parliament. They wanted the conditions for awarding the prize to be "clarified," as they put it. Meaning, altered. And for this to be done legally, Parliament would have to give its approval to a new set of conditions.

Parliament did exactly that. In May of 1765, it passed a bill that changed the rules of the game.

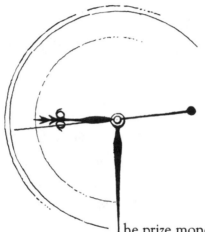

8

·

STILL MORE TRIALS

he prize money was now divided into two parts. Harrison would receive the first half after delivering, under oath, the drawings from which the silver watch was made, along with a written explanation of those drawings. He must also take the watch apart before a group of experts, answering their questions as he did so; then he must surrender the watch, which was to become the property of the nation, along with all three of his earlier clocks.

The second half of the prize money would not be his unless other timekeepers were made that worked as well as the watch. The plural was important here. He must make watches. Not just one, but more than one. The Board required at least two.

These conditions must have brought Harrison close to despair. Hardest of all was the demand that he construct more timekeepers. What would that prove, except that after making one successful watch he was able to make another? Furthermore, the new act said nothing about how these other timekeepers were to be tested, for there was no mention of the West Indies this time, only the vague phrase "upon trial," which could mean anything, however fantastic.

In a letter that was hand-delivered to the Board, Harrison demanded to know why, if the first act was deficient, he had for so long been encouraged under it. And "why was my son sent twice to the West Indies? Had it been said to my son, when he received the last instructions, there will, in case you succeed, be a new Act at your return, in order to lay you under new restrictions, which were not thought of in [that earlier act], I say, had this been the case, I might have expected some such treatment as I now meet with.

"It must be owned that my case is very hard, but I hope I am the first, and for my country's sake shall be the last that suffers by pinning my faith on an English Act of Parliament."

He told them in conclusion that it was better to have solved the longitude problem and go unrewarded than to have "come short of the matter, and by some delusion had the reward."

Upon reading these words, the Board tried to soften their demands about demonstrations of the watch. But Harrison swore he would never consent to them so long as he had a drop of English blood in his body. Then he turned his back on the meeting and stomped out.

According to William's journal, there was another meeting at which his father lost his temper again, threw down a letter in what William described as "an abrupt and scandalous manner," and left. William remained. When asked if he would sign an oath agreeing to take the watch apart before experts, he said he would not, for his father had told him before leaving the building "that he would have nothing further to do with it."

The Board then decided they would have nothing further to do with John Harrison, "till he alters his present sentiments." It was also decided that the minutes of their last four meetings should be published and sold in pamphlet form for sixpence apiece. No doubt the members wanted the man in the street to know their side of the Harrison affair—what they didn't want was for that same ordinary, commonplace man in the street to see the Board of Longitude as so many professors and titled members of the gentry, in the act of bullying another man in the street.

We know nothing about Harrison's state of mind now, his fears and uncertainties; we can only assume that he considered his situation and found it bleak. He was a stubborn man, but the Board of Longitude was equally stubborn and had less to lose.

At last he agreed to the oath, and to dismantling the watch before witnesses. This would be painful, possibly dangerous, since the witnesses might steal all his hard-won secrets. Patent law within the kingdom was unreliable; overseas, there was no legal protection whatever. But painful or not, it had to be done, and he told them he was ready.

Toward the end of May 1765, then, the Board met to work out a procedure for taking the watch apart. There would be six witnesses, they said, including three watchmakers. All six must agree they would never reveal the secrets of the watch to anyone but the Board of Longitude. A seventh witness would go along to supervise: Nevil Maskelyne.

There followed two months of embittered exchanges between the Harrisons and the Board. John Harrison, having said he was ready to sign the oath, was apparently not ready—might never be ready. Thrashing about like a fish caught in the net, he seemed desperate for escape.

At one point William was asked, once and for all, would he or wouldn't he sign? William evaded the question, saying his father couldn't sign because he was unable to understand the meaning of the oath. At this the acting chairman of the Board, Lord Egmont, exclaimed, "Sir, I have told you that we will not hear you talk, for you are the strangest and most obstinate creature that I have ever met with, and, would you do what we want you to do . . . I will give you my word to give you the money if you will but do it."

William agreed, but grudgingly. Speaking for himself, he told them, he was willing to sign. That was all very well, they said, but his father had better sign, too, and not tomorrow or the next day but that very evening.

So they signed the oath, at the same time handing over to the Admiralty the drawings from which the watch was made, with a written explanation of its working parts. And on a Wednesday morning in August, the delegation of seven came to the workshop in Red Lion Square. John Harrison, with William standing by, began taking the silver watch to pieces, setting the pieces on the table, explaining the function of each piece, answering their questions. William's journal has little to say about this procedure. We know only that they were at it Thursday, Friday, and Saturday. Then they stopped for the weekend, and met again on Tuesday and Thursday, at which time they agreed to continue the following week, beginning Monday.

But John Harrison must have had his fill of them already—both the young watchmakers, whom he probably suspected of gobbling up his secrets, and the young Maskelyne, with his bland, somewhat doughy face. Reminding his visitors that the demonstration was supposed to proceed without interruption until everyone was satisfied, Harrison said they'd better come back tomorrow, Friday, rather than wait till Monday.

The committee then decided that they, too, had had enough. The members signed a certificate saying the watch had been fully explained to them, and went away.

A month passed. The Board accepted the signed certificate and

agreed that Harrison would receive the first half of the prize money as soon as he had put the watch back together, and given it—"in perfect condition"—into the hands of the Admiralty, along with the three timekeepers.

Harrison resisted all over again, sometimes angrily, sometimes plaintively, an old man with his back to the wall. He explained that he needed the silver watch in order to make the copies of it that would secure the other half of the prize. But the Board could not be budged. They told him he could keep the three older clocks for now, but the watch had to go.

Once more Harrison gave way. In October of 1765, he surrendered his silver watch to the Board of Longitude. In return, he was given one half of the prize, 10,000 pounds, a handsome amount of money, more than enough to secure the comfort of his wife, his son, and his grandson John, now four years old.

The Board, for reasons of its own, then proceeded to publish all his drawings and explanations, together with the notes made by members of the committee. Harrison felt this to be a mortal blow— as he wrote some time later, they had done it without giving him the second half of the reward, and without "even paying me and my Son for our Time at a rate as common Mechanicks; an Instance of such Cruelty and Injustice as I believe never existed in a learned and civilised Nation before." Fortunately for the Harrisons, the explanations were so poorly written—perhaps intentionally—that they were unlikely to help anyone make a copy of the watch.

News of the award traveled fast, both at home and abroad. Soon other English watchmakers were inspired to design their own seagoing timekeepers. In Paris, it was said that every little French watchmaker was hard at work trying to do the same. What was once an impossible solution to the longitude problem was on its way to becoming practical, even fashionable, and this was all Harrison's doing. By living for years on hope and handouts, while more cautious men built conventional clocks for their customers, he had cleared a path for them.

For the time being, however, the Admiralty had charge of the silver watch, which was sealed up within its box and stuck in a storeroom. It remained there, unused and useless, for a year, leaving Harrison to think over the making of two new watches without the help of the original. And since the Board had never stopped suspecting it was a fluke, on the advice of the Earl of Morton they decided the following spring to take the watch out of storage and send it to the Greenwich Observatory for a series of tests. These tests would be carried out under the supervision of—inevitably—Nevil Maskelyne.

On the fifth of May, that gentleman reported to the Admiralty in the company of Larcum Kendall, a watchmaker, and Captain Thomas Baillie of the Greenwich Hospital, a home for retired sailors situated close by the Observatory. They removed the watch, bore it down a flight of steps and into a barge, then downriver, then up some steps again, until they reached the Observatory. There they placed it in a wooden box with two locks and fastened the box to a seat in the Transit Room. For the next ten months it would be tested against a regulator clock.

Two weeks later, Nevil Maskelyne turned up again at Red Lion Square, this time unannounced. He had with him a letter from the Board that required Harrison to surrender all three older machines, "which are become the property of the Public." They, too, would be taken to the Greenwich Observatory, for which purpose Maskelyne had brought several workmen, as well as two watchmakers. William's journal gives a fairly detailed account of the visit.

Maskelyne demanded to know if the machines were "in perfect order," as stipulated by the Board.

Harrison said he would sign an affidavit to that effect, but only if the Astronomer Royal would do the same.

Maskelyne, the careful administrator, thought this over. He pointed out that he was unable to tell if they were in perfect order— but would agree to state that they were "by all appearances" in perfect order. At about three o'clock, the papers were signed and exchanged.

Next, Maskelyne faced the task of transporting three bulky and sensitive machines from Red Lion Square to the Observatory, a considerable distance. How was he to do it? He asked Harrison for instructions, whether they were usually transported whole or in parts.

Harrison flatly refused to do any instructing. Since Maskelyne was authorized by the Board of Longitude to remove the clocks, he said, it would be quite improper for him, John Harrison, to advise how to do it. And furthermore, he knew perfectly well that if he did give advice, anything that went wrong would be blamed on him.

A Cambridge professor, Roger Long, had come by to help with the negotiations, and at this point he and Maskelyne held a brief conference. Both were infuriated by Harrison's behavior, and Harrison must have been aware of it. He backed down, but not much. He said he usually moved H-2 and H-3 assembled, but H-1 in pieces.

With that he went out, abruptly, marching upstairs to his personal quarters. This was insulting behavior. To insult an Astronomer Royal before a roomful of witnesses was unwise. For one thing, he wasn't there for his own amusement. It was an assignment, an unpleasant one that required him to invade the home of another man, who considered him a villain, and was ill-mannered besides. How did the Astronomer Royal react?

"Mr. Maskelyne with disdain declared although Mr. Harrison would not give any directions or Assistance that he knew as well as Mr. Harrison how to convey [the timekeepers]." This passage comes from a memorandum included in William's journal, and signed by the two watchmakers. Of course, Nevil Maskelyne could not have known how to convey the timekeepers—even if they had been quite ordinary ones, pendulum clocks such as people kept at home, he would not have known how to move them. And these were not ordinary clocks; they were old, massive, and unique.

But Maskelyne had been left with them, and he was going to get the job done. A smith was sent for; when he arrived he brought a pair of pincers. At four o'clock, while H-1 was being taken apart by the smith under Maskelyne's supervision, someone, somehow, "let the same fall, and which we believe broke some of the movements therein at which Mr. Maskelyne's hand was then on the Machine."

H-1 was badly damaged. The two other timekeepers were then "so far abused in the Carriage by Land to Greenwich, as to be rendered quite incorrect," and so far as Harrison could tell, "incapable of being repaired without having some essential Parts made anew." There is no way of knowing if these misadventures were accidental or the result of Maskelyne's being in a foul mood.

The old timepieces play no further role in the Harrison story. But that afternoon of sparring and bickering served to worsen the already strained relations between clockmaker and Astronomer Royal.

All of John Harrison's past had now been taken away from him— the silver watch with great ceremony, the oversize machines like so much miscellaneous baggage—and he was left with the problem of making new timekeepers. During this same period, and after a good deal of backing and filling, the Board finally contracted with Larcum Kendall to create an exact replica of the silver watch. He would begin as soon as the ten-month trial at Greenwich was over.

Whatever happened there, John Harrison was to have no part in it. From start to finish his presence would never be asked for, nor would he offer advice. In Greenwich, as in Red Lion Square, a sullen silence prevailed.

9

IN THE HANDS OF THE ASTRONOMER ROYAL

he Greenwich trial of the silver watch
began in July of 1766, along lines laid out by the Board of Longitude.
Its daily performance was to be compared with the observatory's regulator clock and the results faithfully recorded. Two witnesses must
be present each day, an officer of the Royal Greenwich Hospital and
either Maskelyne or one of his assistants. There were two locks on
the box containing the watch. The keys to one lock were to be held
by the governor of the Hospital; those to the other, by Maskelyne.
Therefore it could never be wound, adjusted, or even peeked at by
Maskelyne alone.

For most of the test period the watch was to lie face up, in a horizontal position, and this leads us to one of the minor mysteries connected with the trial. John Harrison had used gimbals—a sling arrangement that keeps an instrument level—for his sea clocks, but refused to use them with the watch. No one knew his reasons then, and they are still unknown. When the silver watch first went to sea, he insisted that it must lie between two cushions within its box; William kept it more or less horizontal by frequent adjustments, using such simple devices as a marble in a bowl—when the marble rests motionless at the bottom, the bowl is level.

Now the Board wanted to see how well the watch endured the motions of an oceangoing ship without William's tender care. They told Maskelyne to try it in a variety of positions, faceup, facedown, and tilted—quite sharply tilted. This part of the test was to last about six weeks. When the trial was completed, results would be published in book form and made available to the public. There were to be no interim reports, however, so the Harrisons would have no way of telling how the watch performed day by day.

Halfway through the test period, John learned that James, the brother he had once collaborated with, who was eleven years younger, had died in Barrow-upon-Humber. The first issue of Maskelyne's brainchild, *The Nautical Almanac*, was published a month or so later. And in March of 1767, an account of the Greenwich trial appeared in print, price two shillings and sixpence.

Eighty pages long, dense with figures and tables, the thrust of its meaning shone like a knife blade in Maskelyne's introduction: "That

Mr. Harrison's watch cannot be depended upon to keep the Longitude within a degree in a West India voyage of six weeks; nor to keep the longitude within half a degree for more than a few days; and perhaps not so long, if the cold be very intense; nevertheless, that it is a useful and valuable invention, and, in conjunction with the observations of the distance of the moon from the sun and fixed stars, may be of considerable advantage to navigation."

So this was what it had come to: the surrender of his much loved watch, of the drawings, of all three ancient timekeepers, was now capped by a public declaration that the watch wasn't up to much after all, undependable on its own, at best a useful invention when coupled with lunars.

John Harrison sprang to the defense of his watch and his prize. At the age of seventy-four, he can hardly have wanted the rest of the money for himself. What was it he wanted?

John Milton writes about fame as "That last infirmity of noble mind." Surely this was what Harrison cared for most: fame, reputation, the acknowledgement by a grateful nation that a watch could fix the longitude, and not just any watch—it must be his, the one that Almighty God had permitted him to complete. With James Short as his ghostwriter, he fired off a pamphlet in reply to Maskelyne. Its tone was accusatory. Instead of pointing to the all-important truth that the watch had already proved its accuracy—on shipboard, and in the opinion of experts—he aimed to destroy every shred of Maskelyne's argument along with Maskelyne himself.

The watch had been exposed to the wildest extremes of heat and

In the Hands of the Astronomer Royal

cold, he said, which damaged its temperature curb. During the time it was locked inside a glass-covered box in the Transit Room, the glass turned the box into a miniature greenhouse—while all along the temperature was being monitored by a thermometer in a different part of the room, well shaded and cool. As for the experiments in position, they were meaningless. The watch was never adjusted for those positions, since no motions of a ship would require it. The officers of the Greenwich Hospital were not reliable witnesses to Nevil Maskelyne's doings; they were old, lame, hardly able to climb the hill that led to the Observatory, and they were so timidly respectful of the Astronomer Royal that they signed their names to whatever he wanted. Also, the locks on the box in which the watch was kept could be picked with a crooked nail; anyone might have tampered with them.

The charges continue: Maskelyne had drawn all the wrong conclusions from the data, his lunar method wasn't much use to begin with, and in any case he was interested in lunars "in a pecuniary way"—meaning he wanted the prize for himself.

Nevil Maskelyne made no reply to Harrison's pamphlet. He could have explained that it was nonsense to say he wanted the prize for himself, since he had never applied for any sort of reward under the Longitude Act, neither the first nor the second. He had requested that an award of money be sent to Tobias Mayer's widow, which was granted, but he asked for nothing himself.

Yet there is little doubt that Maskelyne's findings were very strange indeed, certainly hard to understand in the face of the watch's previous performance.

The likeliest explanation is a simple one. Harrison had taken the watch apart in his workroom, with the two watchmakers and Maskelyne looking on. After they left, it was reassembled, but was not prepared for further tests. Then the Admiralty swooped down and carried it off to its storehouse, and then to Greenwich, where it was placed under glass and overheated. Yet Maskelyne conducted his tests with rigor, without making allowances for the delicacy of the instrument, without ever inquiring about rate.

If Harrison and the Astronomer Royal had been on cordial terms, if anything like normal communication had existed between Greenwich and Red Lion Square, the story might have been different.

Now Harrison was wounded and bleeding, while Maskelyne remained proudly silent. And the Board of Longitude, whose most influential member was Maskelyne, treated Harrison with a harshness it is hard to justify. The silver watch was in Larcum Kendall's hands; when Harrison asked if he could have it, even briefly, to help in the creation of Number Five, the Board told him that was out of the question because Kendall needed it.

Five weeks later, at a meeting John Harrison attended, the Board announced plans for the testing of his new watches, the two he must produce to win the second half of the prize. Nothing so straightforward as a voyage to the West Indies this time. First, a ten-month trial at the Greenwich Observatory, "and in case of the natural heat of the season in the place where the said timekeepers shall be kept . . . does not arise to 86 degrees Fahrenheit, an artificial heat be applied sufficient to raise the thermometer to that degree." Then a two-month trial aboard ship, perhaps one anchored in a turbulent stretch of the English Channel. Or else in Hudson Bay. The Board refused to say how accurately the watches must perform during these ordeals.

The original act of Parliament was still in force, requiring a trial of some six weeks' length, but now the Board was talking about a year's worth of tests. It was an outrageous demand.

At that point a lesser man than Harrison might have given up. His eyesight was failing, his hands were no longer steady; how could he perform this most exacting kind of work without reliable hands and eyes? How could he meet standards that the Board refused to reveal? Stubborn as ever, he simply disappeared into his workshop to start on Number Five. It could not be done, but he would do it.

William was not hopeful. He would try everything, he said in a letter to a relative—"I will not leave one stone unturned"—while expecting nothing. In William's opinion, he and his father had such powerful opponents that they must resign themselves to defeat.

Larcum Kendall, meanwhile, brought his exact copy of the silver watch before the Board. It was pronounced a fine piece of work; even William said so. The Board wondered how it was that Kendall had already finished the copy while Harrison continued to make excuses about delays and difficulties connected with Number Five.

Kendall even offered to build a simplified version of the silver watch, cheaper than the original, and more quickly made. And John Arnold, a talented young watchmaker, who had presented the King with a repeating watch so small it was set in a finger ring, told the Board he could make a longitude watch for about sixty pounds. Both these men were far easier to deal with than Harrison, by now a thorn in the Board's collective side.

Harrison must have heard of Arnold's doings as well as Kendall's, and hurried his adjustments to the new watch. He could not compete with cheap, simplified workmanship, and he had exhausted his bargaining power with the Board of Longitude. Yet he knew he must demonstrate that H-4 was no fluke, and the only way to do it was by making a second such watch that would perform equally well.

It was the Board, in the person of Nevil Maskelyne, that would do the testing and evaluate the performance. And it was the Board and only the Board that would pronounce the final verdict. But Harrison no longer trusted the Board and had been convinced for some time that Maskelyne was his sworn enemy. What was he to do? Where was he to turn? He probably discussed these matters with friends and advisers.

When H-5 was finished, in early 1772, it was much the same as the silver watch, although without the elegant piercing and engraving. Harrison had now reached the age of seventy-nine. His chances of living long enough to make still another such watch were surely remote. Yet if he didn't make this other watch, he would lose not only the prize itself, but what he valued far more, fame and immortality and being known as the man who conquered longitude. The great question remained: how to be sure of fair treatment, how to bypass the treacherous Board of Longitude. Was there anyone in England powerful enough to take his side against them?

The choice he finally made was outrageously bold, although at the same time almost obvious. He would enlist the help of His Majesty King George III.

10

"FARMER GEORGE"

he story of Harrison and George III has some
of the elements of a fairy tale; it seems unlikely, far-fetched. But the
King in this case was a very real person, and the broad outlines of
the narrative are recorded in papers of the Board and elsewhere.

When it comes to the details, however, those that show the King
and the watch from close-up, there is indeed a fairy-tale quality. This
aspect of the story comes from a document titled *Memoirs of a Trait
in the Character of George III*. The author's name is given as Johan
Horrins, which is an anagram for John Harrison—the grandson of

John Harrison the watchmaker. And we learn from Humphrey Quill, the biographer of our Harrison, that Horrins was "an extremely odd and even mysterious character about whom all too little is known." What's more, some years after publication of the memoirs all trace of the original disappeared.

But Horrins-Harrison was as real as the King and the watchmaker, and historians take his account essentially at face value because it fits with known events. As for the character of the King as he appears here, he has been abundantly written about—partly because it was during his reign that revolution exploded in America and a new country was born. Different biographers have somewhat different versions, of course, but there is general agreement about the main themes.

When the story of the King and John Harrison begins, George III was in his mid-thirties. Upon coming to the throne twelve years earlier, he had addressed Parliament with the following words: "Born and educated in this country, I glory in the name of Briton." So he did, in marked contrast to his royal ancestors, for the two previous Georges had been German-born; they spoke poor English or none at all, and they took every opportunity to escape to the country of their birth, where life was better, finer, purer. This new George spoke like an Englishman.

Fatherless since the age of twelve, he had been desperately shy as a boy, and as a young man he was still shy, also obstinate, self-righteous, and a poor judge of character. But he kept his feelings of inadequacy to himself, although they troubled him deeply. What the country at large saw was a tall, dignified, pleasant-looking gentleman with ruddy cheeks and a steady, open expression. He was young, twenty-three at the time of his coronation, and England had not had such a young monarch since the sixteenth century.

Now, in 1772, the King's personal tastes and interests were taking shape. He had an active mind, a lively curiosity. The things he cared about most included farm animals and all forms of modern agriculture, for which he earned the affectionate nickname "Farmer George." He collected enormous numbers of books, not because he loved books but because he respected them. He was interested in the arts; he played the harpsichord and loved opera and anything composed by Handel. He went to the theater often with his German-born wife, and they enjoyed nothing so much as a good comedy. George had a poor opinion of Shakespeare, however, although he knew "one must not say so!"

He was known to be warmhearted. Where the two earlier Georges had been pompous, this one took a friendly interest in ordinary, everyday people. When living in the country at Windsor, he would go about from one small house to another to watch people at work, talking with them, asking questions about how they lived, these questions punctuated with the rapid-fire "What, what, what!" that was his trademark.

He was not, of course, a believer in democracy, in the idea that all people are created equal. He knew it was right and just for the nation to be governed by its hereditary aristocracy. But he was honest, genuine, and approachable. And this may have been one of the reasons that John Harrison turned to him as the powerful protector who could take his part against the Board of Longitude.

There was another, even stronger reason. George was the first British monarch to be educated in science. He had no deep knowledge of science himself—"I do not pretend to any superior abilities," he said—but he invited scientists to Windsor to show him their experiments. He collected such scientific instruments as microscopes, telescopes, barometers, working models of engines, and serious toys that demonstrated the powers of magnetism.

Furthermore, the King was an amateur astronomer, a fairly serious one. He was familiar with Edmond Halley's writings about the transit of Venus, and they inspired him to have an observatory built for his personal use.

It was known that the planet Venus passes directly between earth and sun twice in slightly more than a century, the two events, or transits, being eight years apart. And while the transit is taking place—a matter of several hours—Venus can be seen in silhouette against the bright solar disk. Halley had pointed out in 1716 that observing such a transit would provide a way of measuring one of the basic units of astronomy, the distance between earth and sun. From this the dimensions of the solar system would be learned. Although Halley longed to see the next transits himself, in 1761 and 1769, he knew he would be gone by then, so he urged all "diligent searchers of the Heavens . . . to apply themselves actively and with all their might to making the necessary observations."

The King did as Halley suggested. There was already the official observatory at Greenwich, home and headquarters of the Astronomer Royal, but George wanted one of his own, and in 1768, in plenty of time for the second transit, an observatory was built for him at Richmond. The king's boyhood tutor in science, Dr. Stephen Demainbray, became its director.

George was proud of his observatory, took pleasure in showing it off to visitors, and sometimes hung his hat over the roof telescope when some royal personage was in the act of examining the heavens. His sense of humor was as simple and direct as the man himself.

Best of all—perhaps the surest sign that the King would come to the Harrisons' rescue—he took a particular interest in timekeepers. He had rewarded John Arnold handsomely for the finger ring with a watch set in it, and after commissioning an elaborate and costly clock, he helped design the face. He had even worked on watches himself, and published directions for taking apart and reassembling a watch.

The Harrisons knew he would not be able to right their wrongs with a single stroke of the pen, since he was not an absolute monarch—absolute monarchy had ended the century before, when Charles I was beheaded. But the King still held certain significant powers. He controlled the appointment of cabinet ministers, for example, and was therefore able to influence individual members of Parliament.

The Harrisons decided to approach him by way of Dr. Demainbray. Early in 1772, William sent off a long letter describing his father's years of work on longitude clocks, and how all went well until the finish of the first sea trial to Jamaica, after which the Board turned against his father, even introducing a new law, with the result that he was now being "brow-beaten by one set of men, and betrayed by another." But with the King's gracious help in testing H-5 at Richmond, "I should hope that the prejudices of many might thereby be vanquished."

Demainbray's reaction must have been a favorable one, for the King summoned William to Windsor and questioned him at length. According to the memoirs, the King heard him out and remarked in an undertone, "These people have been cruelly treated." Then, turning to William: "By God, Harrison, I will see you righted!"

To begin with, there would be a test period six weeks long, in the Richmond observatory, carried out by Dr. Demainbray, and under the King's personal supervision. The clock would be kept in a box with three locks, one key apiece to be held by His Majesty, Demainbray, and William. They would meet in the observatory every day at noon, unlock the watch box, and compare H-5 with a regulator clock; then H-5 would be wound and put back in the box. The whole procedure was almost identical to the trial of the silver watch on its voyages to the West Indies, but with an important difference: John Harrison, waiting at home for William's return at the end of the day, would hear daily reports.

For three days running, the news was disastrous. According to Horrins, H-5 "was found to have erred to a degree that would have rendered it useless for its intended purpose." It is not hard to imagine the humiliation John Harrison suffered, his sense that all was utterly, finally lost. Yet all was not lost. On the fourth day, the grandson's account continues. "His Majesty, on a sudden recollection exclaimed 'he had found it out'; and . . . he hastened himself to open the door of a closet in the apartment, where appeared three most powerful combinations of lodestones . . . the effect of which left so unlooked for a disappointment no longer a mystery."

The anecdote is a curious one. Lodestones are rocks of iron ore that possess magnetic properties—but the magnetic strength of iron ore is considerably less than that of the modern bar magnet. The lodestones would have had to be only inches away from the watch to interfere with it, and under such conditions it hardly seems credible that they were not noticed earlier.

Nevertheless, the grandson insists that as soon as the King removed them, the watch recovered. For the rest of the six weeks' trial its performance was so admirable that the King proposed two more weeks, then a further two weeks, to make absolutely certain of convincing the Board.

During this time the three holders of keys met every day in the informal atmosphere of the Richmond observatory. William's journal came to an end several years earlier, and the grandson never describes these meetings. We are therefore left to wonder how William conducted himself, how much of his "decidedly objectionable character" was revealed to the King.

William took no interest in science or clocks, and after his father's

King George III and H-5

death he had nothing to do with timekeepers of any sort. So far as is known, he had no particular interests whatever, except helping his father win the prize that he, William, would inherit. What did they talk about?

Maybe there was no opportunity for talk; the King might have appeared for the daily clock-winding and then disappeared. It's also possible that he enjoyed William's company, for this was the King who liked hearing about the doings of ordinary people. However it happened, by the time the trial was over, William and George were not only allies but in a sense co-conspirators, and this may have made a difference to John Harrison's fate.

The Harrisons now put together a memorandum describing the test at Richmond and what it showed: four and a half seconds lost in ten weeks. The document was presented to the Board of Longitude, and the Board of Longitude was not impressed. Scholars, political figures, and men of science, its members were also freeborn Englishmen and entitled to act as they thought best, no matter what any Highness said or did. The trial at Richmond was an unofficial one; any trial not under the Board of Longitude's thumb was unofficial. Besides, two new timekeepers of John Arnold's were ready for testing, and Larcum Kendall was eager to start on his cut-rate chronometer. Until the Board knew how well these rival watches performed, it was not about to listen to the Harrisons—was by now thoroughly fed up with the pair of them. The memorandum was rejected.

John Harrison, in turn, had long since given up on the Board. He put his hopes in Parliament instead, and in the King. As William wrote to a relative, "I have an opportunity to lay before His Majesty every Tuesday everything which I have done, and I do not write one word or take one step without acquainting him with it."

Meanwhile, far from England, on shipboard, and under the extremest conditions of heat and cold, a watch-machine of Harrison's design was undergoing the most practical of tests. Captain James Cook had taken it with him on his second great voyage of exploration.

11

ABOARD THE *RESOLUTION*

A friend of Captain Cook's widow claimed that before her death she destroyed all her husband's letters to her, and did it so thoroughly that nowhere in her house was there a single piece of paper with his handwriting on it—as far as she was concerned, private life was private.

Cook was a public figure, however, who lived very much in the public eye. His shipboard logs and journals survive, as do journals and memoirs kept by some of the men who sailed with him, for he was widely written about and talked about. So while his innermost thoughts and motivations remain unknown, his actions, especially his personal style, do his speaking for him.

Contemporary portraits show a tall man, strongly built and striking in appearance, with a natural air of authority. He was said to be practical and matter-of-fact. At the same time, he had certain ideas and ideals that were very much his own and that differed considerably from those of other naval commanders. For example, it was a strict rule with Cook that when there was any serious shortage of food aboard ship, whatever supplies they had must be distributed evenly, share and share alike, to everyone from captain to cabin boy. The traditions of the Royal Navy were not based on a belief that the life of a cabin boy was equal in value to the life of a captain.

Cook was not a gentleman by birth, as were most officers; in fact, his background was far humbler than John Harrison's. His father had been a migrant laborer, illiterate and without skills, who found steady work with a Yorkshire farmer. James was born on the farm in 1728; thanks to the generosity of his father's employer, he was able to attend a village school until the age of twelve.

At eighteen he apprenticed himself to a shipowner in the port of Whitby and learned his seamanship on the sturdy, coal-carrying ships that sailed the treacherous waters of the North Sea. Some ten years later he volunteered for the Royal Navy, with the rating of able seaman. Everything he knew about surveying, astronomy, and mathematics he had taught himself.

His superiors recognized his talents, and he rose through the ranks, saw active service during the Seven Years' War, and later helped survey the coast of what he called the Island of New-foundland. While there, he observed an eclipse of the sun, an event of such interest to him that he sent a detailed account to the Royal Society. This was an unusual project for a man without a commission; commissions were traditionally reserved for those who had taken care to be born into good families, and he was still rated only as "master."

Luckily for Cook and for England, the Royal Society kept an open mind in these matters; its members were mostly well born and well educated, yet they knew that thinking men could be found in every walk of life. In 1768 they needed a capable navigator, one who could take a ship to the little-known waters of the South Pacific and supervise astronomical observations there. At any rate, this was the official version. There were other orders, described in secret papers.

Officially, and under the sponsorship of the Royal Society, the expedition would be sailing for Tahiti in order to witness the 1769 transit of Venus. Observations of the 1761 transit had been troubled by cloudy skies; now scientists from all over Europe prepared for their second chance, knowing that more than a century must pass before there was another.

The secret orders came from the Admiralty, and its goal was political: to explore the southern seas in search of undiscovered lands and claim them for the Crown. It was widely believed that a great continent existed somewhere in the Southern Hemisphere, one large enough to balance the landmasses of the Northern Hemisphere. The true purpose of the expedition was to find it.

This was how James Cook, an obscure member of the King's navy, skilled at navigation and with an interest in astronomy, came to make his first voyage of exploration. Hurriedly commissioned—a modest commission, as lieutenant—he was allowed to choose his ship. He wanted a stout coal carrier made in the Whitby yards, and one was refitted for him and christened HMS *Endeavour*. The Royal Society told him that their delegation would be headed by Joseph Banks, a young gentleman and enthusiastic naturalist. Banks brought aboard with him two artists, four servants, a secretary, and two dogs. They sailed for Tahiti in 1768, observed the transit of Venus, then began an extensive exploration of the South Pacific.

Using lunar-distance calculations for the longitude, Cook surveyed and charted all of New Zealand and claimed it for the Crown. He surveyed the entire east coast of Australia, two thousand miles long, and successfully crossed the Great Barrier Reef, one of the world's worst threats to navigation. Joseph Banks collected thousands of plant specimens that no one in England had ever seen, and three years after their departure they were home again.

London went wild with excitement over Banks, the newspapers were full of Mr. Banks and Mr. Banks's voyage, noble and fashionable people called at his handsome house and exclaimed over his botanical specimens. Oxford offered an honorary degree.

James Cook, who was neither young nor rich, had a more modest reception, but he was received at court, and he gave King George a firsthand explanation of the voyage and the charts. The King responded by handing Cook his new commission as commander; this was an unheard-of honor for a man of his background, made possible largely through Lord Anson's reforms of the promotion process in the Royal Navy. After a year ashore, surrounded by the comforts of home and family, Cook could hardly wait to set sail again.

The Royal Society had sponsored the first voyage. The second was to be sponsored by the Board of Longitude, the chief mission this time being geographical. Cook would go due south to begin the first exploration of the Antarctic, and he would continue to search for the southern landmass, the one that so surely existed in a temperate climate.

Again, there was a secondary purpose. Nevil Maskelyne requested the Admiralty's help in furnishing Cook with "Astronomical Instruments . . . and also some of the Longitude Watches." He had tested H-4 and found it wanting, he fully believed in the superior claims of the lunar method, but everyone was talking about watches now. Cheap watches. Maskelyne was ready to have some of these new watches tested by Cook. Three of Arnold's were chosen to go, and the Kendall replica of the silver watch. The Board told the Harrisons that if H-5 was ready in time, it could go as well.

But John Harrison was aware that the voyage would take several years, and he could not bring himself to part with H-5. He had hardly finished the work of testing it; suppose he died before he got it back? Together with William, he appealed to the Board to send H-4, the original silver watch—he was ready, he said, to stake his claim to the rest of the prize on its performance with Cook, or to submit "to any mode of trial, by men not already proved partial."

Impossible. The Board refused to allow the silver watch out of the country. They also reminded Harrison that H-5 wasn't enough, that he must produce a total of two new watches. It was a chilling reply and a cruel one, and must have been influenced by Kendall's recent work on cut-rate versions of H-4. As it turned out, while these were simpler, cheaper, and faster to make, they were also greatly inferior, but the Board knew this only later. The final decision was for Kendall's replica of the silver watch to go with Cook, while the genuine article remained safely at home.

In the summer of 1772, and as the King's trial of H-5 drew to a close, Cook made ready to sail from Plymouth. He would have two ships this time, the *Adventure* and the *Resolution*, each equipped with an astronomer and instruments. The four watch-machines would travel two to a ship in boxes specially made for them, each box with its three locks and three keys, and elaborate instructions for the daily winding.

But Cook took little interest in watch-machines, no matter who designed them. His journals make clear that he was all for lunars and Maskelyne. *The Nautical Almanac* would guide the second voyage, just as earlier editions had guided the first. And almost every detail of the watch-machine tests had been planned and managed by the Royal Society—meaning Nevil Maskelyne. He was the one who chose the astronomers. He wrote up lists of the necessary instruments and helped obtain them. Procedures for testing the clocks were his as well; they were to be given a fair trial against his own method, but the trial would be as severe as Nevil Maskelyne could decently make it.

When equipment was loaded onto the ships, the boxes holding Harrison-Kendall and Arnold's Number Three were put in Cook's cabin aboard the *Resolution*, Arnold's first and second going to the *Adventure*. Other supplies that came on board were provided by the Admiralty in its campaign against scurvy. Still others were due to Cook's interest in the welfare of that lowest form of naval life, Jack Tar, the ordinary seaman.

Cook insisted on absolute cleanliness, everywhere. The decks, the cabins, and the space where sailors slept and ate had to be regularly scrubbed clean with vinegar, and vinegar was taken aboard by the barrelful. These same areas were to be kept well ventilated, which meant airing them out once or twice a week, either by fumigation with a mixture of gunpowder and vinegar or by firing up stoves, and this was done even in the hottest weather.

Personal cleanliness was encouraged, and enforced by example— cold bathing, the regular washing of hands before meals, the changing of wet clothes. Such behavior was foreign to sailors, even repulsive, but it was Cook's belief that their health depended on it. He had been known to punish men for coming to meals with dirty hands.

They could be punished for refusing to eat fresh meat, for it was another of his convictions that a diet of fresh meat, eggs, and quantities of green stuff would protect them from scurvy. This was generally known to sailors of his time, although they had no way of knowing that vitamin C, ascorbic acid, was the magical substance; nor did they know that prolonged cooking destroys vitamin C. All the same, seagoing men were aware that if a ship was supplied with certain kinds of food, there would be no scurvy aboard.

Long voyages were another matter. When the *Centurion* circled the globe under Anson's command, months went by without even a glimpse of land. During those months there was no green stuff to be had, and sailors died by the hundreds.

Now the Admiralty was experimenting with foods that could survive a long voyage—orange syrups, for example, and quantities of a German preparation called "sour krout." Hoping that these would work as scurvy preventives, it gave Cook enough sauerkraut to supply seventy men with two pounds of it every week for a year. On the first voyage, his sailors had been willing to eat the sweet syrups but refused even to taste the sauerkraut, which they considered foreign and therefore disgusting. Cook had it served up every day in the officers' mess; his journal notes that he "permitted all the officers without exception to make use of it and left it to the option of the Men either to take as much as they pleased or none at all." Soon they were tasting it, and in time became accustomed to it.

When ashore, he ordered them to gather and eat "almost Every Herb Plant Root and kinds of Fruit they Could Possibly Light upon," as one of the men put it. They were also to eat whatever fresh meat they could lay hands on. He himself had set an example in Tahiti by having a dinner of baked dog; in Antarctica, it would be penguin.

As it happened, the orange syrups were useless against scurvy, since they had been boiled. Sauerkraut, on the other hand—pickled rather than cooked—was effective, as were the greens, and every kind of fresh meat, including penguin.

It's worth noting that Dr. James Lind, a naval surgeon, had learned as early as 1753 that citrus fruits were a scurvy preventive. For some reason, the Admiralty ignored Lind's findings, and Cook knew nothing about them—which makes it all the more remarkable that Nevil Maskelyne took three gallons of lemon juice aboard when he sailed to St. Helena in 1761.

Of all the health measures used by Captain Cook, the most powerful was surely his character. He took the trouble to do something about the men's welfare, and to do it personally. He enforced, he insisted, he persuaded by example. When supervision was needed—and getting British seamen to bathe every day in cold salt water would have required constant supervision—he gave it. Yet he did not treat his men gently. He was strict with them, at times harsh. There were floggings aboard his ships, although not often; he was a naval officer, he needed some means of punishment, and flogging was the standard practice. What was remarkable about Cook was his decency, his essential humaneness. In the eighteenth century, these qualities were not considered the foremost of manly virtues.

In July of 1772, then, stocked with sauerkraut, vinegar, nautical instruments and portable tent-observatories and the four seagoing watches, as well as all the usual supplies, the two ships set sail. They headed south, crossed the equator, and continued south past the Cape of Good Hope, and into the unknown waters of the Antarctic Ocean.

It was December by the time they got there, almost midsummer. The weather was terrifying. Although the men were well and warmly dressed in garments called fearnoughts, in order to handle the rigging their hands had to be bare. The ropes were frozen through and through. Frostbite—sometimes followed by amputation—was a constant danger. Blizzards lashed the two ships; mountainous icebergs, some two miles in circumference and two hundred feet high, threatened to sink them. They escaped by steering east, south of Australia to the southern tip of New Zealand.

The next seven months were spent in the generally calmer waters of the South Pacific. Whenever they planned to be in one place for any length of time, the astronomers rushed ashore with their equipment. The observatory-tents were set up, telescopes and other instruments were installed inside them, and pendulum clocks were given several days to calm down. After the astronomers found correct local time by means of equal altitudes, they set the pendulum clocks accordingly, and used them from then on as regulator clocks.

Now, with the help of quadrants and the clocks, the error of every watch-machine could be found. One of the Arnolds went badly from the start. Another stopped entirely. The third was doing well enough—"not to be complained on," Cook noted—although it lost at an increasing rate. The Harrison-Kendall gave no trouble at all.

But Cook had not changed his mind. So far as he was concerned, lunars were still the best solution to the longitude problem. They were modern, scientific. With Maskelyne's *Nautical Almanac*, Cook could complete a lunar calculation in fifteen minutes, and believed all naval men should do the same. Few of them had Cook's nimble mind, however, or his head for mathematics. They would give up dead reckoning only when they had something simpler and more direct in its place.

The Harrison-Kendall timekeeper ticked steadily on, day and night, and its information could be had almost at a glance. It needed daily winding, it needed clear weather so that local time could be established by the sun's altitude—but otherwise it made no demands. And halfway through the voyage, Cook began to see it for the treasure it was. He called it "our trusty friend the Watch," and "our faithful guide."

The two ships headed south again, crossed the Antarctic Circle until stopped by unbroken pack ice, then changed course, to explore the scattered islands of the South Pacific. By this time the Harrison-

95
90
85
80
75
70
65
60
55
50

Captain Cook and K-1

Kendall watch had endured every kind of weather, from tropical humidity and torrential rain to hail, sleet, furious gales, and blinding Antarctic fog, and it never once failed.

Cook's greatest act of faith in it took place near the end of the voyage, as they sailed north from the Cape of Good Hope, headed for the island of St. Helena; the *Dutton*, a ship of the East India Company, sailed with them. Cook planned to make straight for his goal this time—"Depending on the goodness of [the Harrison-Kendall watch] I resolved to try to make the island by a direct course," as the journal has it. The captain of the *Dutton* was nervous about this. He would have preferred the usual, indirect approach, finding the island's latitude, then sailing the parallel until they sighted land. Suppose they missed it altogether?

But Cook did as he planned; the watch "did not deceive us and we made it accordingly . . . at Day-break." The commercial advantage of being able to steer direct was not lost on the *Dutton*'s captain; within a very few years the Company began equipping its fleet with seagoing watches.

As the three-year voyage drew to a close, one of the astronomers sent a report to the Admiralty that ended with these words: "From the preceding account it appears to what an amazing degree of accuracy the ingenious Inventor of this Watch had brought this branch of mechanics so long ago as the year 1762 . . . let no man boast that he has excelled him, until his machines have undergone as rigorous a trial as this has done." An officer of the *Resolution* claimed the watch was nothing less than "the greatest piece of Mechanism the world has yet produced."

When he reached England again in 1775, Cook would report that his ship had been scurvy-free. He brought news of the great southern continent, namely, that it did not exist. And he had with him the first charts of the South Sea Islands, wonderfully accurate ones thanks to his "trusty friend the Watch."

For whatever the Board of Longitude believed or claimed to believe about the performance of the silver watch, this voyage would prove it was no fluke.

Cook's return was still in the future as John Harrison, having handed all his affairs over to William, waited, without hope, for an end to the long business of the prize. He made no attempt to train apprentices; he showed no interest in having his technology preserved for posterity. He was increasingly pessimistic.

"Nonsense, Spite and Poison (scandalously scurvy, dirty Work indeed) as runs throughout the Whole of their maliciously groundless Objections, as objecting against Things which are really true and done," he wrote about his opponents. They were people whose social or academic positions gave them the right to stand in judgment of his work, which in his opinion they did not, could not understand.

William continued to place his hopes in the advice and counsel of the King. He addressed a letter to the most powerful man in England, Lord North, the Prime Minister; this was surely done at the King's suggestion. Six months later he sent another long letter to John Robinson, Secretary of the Treasury. Nothing came of either appeal, so in April of 1773 William turned to the House of Commons, submitting a petition that asked for justice and the second half of the prize money.

Parliament began to stir itself. It instructed the Board of Longitude to meet and "revise their proceedings in relation to the said Mr. Harrison." Two members of Parliament who had taken an interest in the Harrison case were told to be present at the Board's next meeting, to ensure that Parliament understood the goings-on. This made the Board so uneasy that seven Admiralty clerks were set to work day and night, copying out the Board's resolutions concerning the Harrisons, which would then be printed and made available to the public. The Board was still wary of the man in the street, who was so likely to identify with Harrison.

Other events took place at the same time. The Board summoned William Harrison and bombarded him with questions: Would his father make two other timekeepers and submit them to be tried? If the Board appointed two or more persons, to whom William had no objection, to make this trial, would he agree to it? If not, why not? William answered no to everything.

On April 27 the petition to Parliament was debated in the House of Commons, and speeches were made, both for and against. One who supported Harrison was the brilliant young Irishman Edmund

Burke, whose defense of the American colonists was considered so biting and witty that even those on the other side of the House— the government side—were unable to stop laughing.

Now Burke demanded to know why a man of Harrison's advanced age "is to make new watches . . . Good God, Sir, can this be a British House of Commons? This most ingenious and able mechanic, who has spent above 40 years of an industrious and valuable life in search of this great discovery—and has discovered it; who has, according to the verdict of the whole mechanical world, done more than ever was expected . . . to have his legal right withheld from him . . . Is this a conduct worthy of the munificence of this House? Of a nation that owes to her navigation her wealth, her consequence, her fame?"

In spite of lively debate, no conclusion was reached. And in the meanwhile the Harrisons' advisers, including the King, told them they would do better by withdrawing the petition and wording it differently. They believed the Board was within its rights in refusing the rest of the prize money—the Board had been harsh, perhaps extremely harsh, these advisers maintained, but on strictly legal grounds the gentlemen of the Board could not be faulted.

The Harrisons saw they would have to put their pleas on a personal basis. Forgetting all that had gone before, they must rest their claims on John Harrison's accomplishment in having made a timekeeper that determined longitude at sea—and in having spent a lifetime at the task, so that he was now too old to fulfill the remaining conditions.

He was far too old; he had just turned eighty. As the Admiralty's seven clerks continued their copying, a second petition was drawn up. Its opening words, like a trumpet flourish, made known to the Commons that "His Majesty, having been informed of the Contents of the said Petition, recommended it to the Consideration of the House." The King had already told William he was willing, if necessary, to appear before the House and give his personal testimony in John Harrison's favor. It was an extraordinary offer, a tribute to "this most ingenious and able mechanic," the former village carpenter, and also to the generous nature of George III.

Fortunately for both of them, the King had no need to appear. Parliament responded to the revised petition by drawing up a money bill in record time, awarding what amounted to the second half of the prize money. The King consented. The bill was passed.

John Harrison had proved himself more than a match for those he called the priests and professors. He had fought his fight and won it—but he had not won the prize itself. He had been given an amount of money equal to it, as a reward for a lifetime's worth of research, but there was no certificate, no proclamation, no announcement to the world that he had solved the longitude problem. In that sense, nobody ever won the great prize.

These were only details to the public at large. In their eyes, Harrison had emerged triumphant: the King was on his side; the money was in his hand; the "Men of Theory" had done their utmost against him and failed. Three more years were left to him, and he

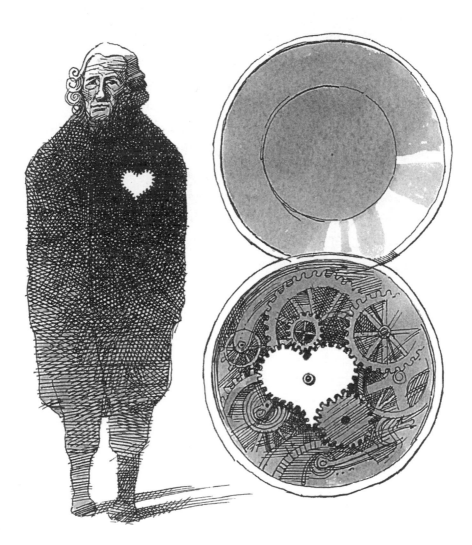

spent them in the house at Red Lion Square, suffering badly from gout, but still working. He worked as he always had, for the love of it, and because his brain dreamed clockmaking. William's son tells us that, in old age, John Harrison had little interest in anything but his family and his clocks. He had partly constructed a clock that he believed would vary by no more than one second in a hundred days.

He died on March 24, 1776, his eighty-third birthday. Cook had returned to England in July of 1775, and although we can't be sure that Harrison heard about the great success of the watch, it's highly likely that word came to him somehow. He would have seen it as a total vindication of his life's work, a proof that he had finally achieved what he most longed for, his rightful place in history.

AFTERWARD

By the end of the eighteenth century navigators were finding longitude by using the two methods together, checking a watch-machine against lunars, and lunars by the watch-machine. But the time-keeping system was so much more practical that interest in lunars gradually fell away. Navigators would take along several watch-machines—they had come to be called marine chronometers—and check them against one another. And by the start of the twentieth century lunars were a thing of the past, of interest only to antiquarians.

Some Harrison inventions survive into modern times, the

bimetallic strip, for example, while others were too delicate to be successful in any hands but his own. He had built the most accurate pendulum clocks the world had ever seen; he had recognized the damaging effects of friction on timekeepers and found ingenious ways of reducing friction; he had created two original and effective devices to compensate for changes in temperature; and in designing the silver watch, he had shown that for a portable timekeeper to work efficiently aboard ship, it must have at its heart a small balance beating rapidly. Once he showed it could be done, others were able to follow in his footsteps, without the heartache of a lifetime's uncertain labor.

Navigation was safer after Harrison, not only because ships knew where they were but because they could be supplied with accurate maps. There are people who claim that the growth and prosperity of the British Empire were partly built on Harrison timekeepers.

In succeeding centuries, machine production of clocks and watches has made them smaller, cheaper, and—with the advent of electric clocks, either battery-powered or line-powered—highly accurate. A discovery by Pierre Curie, that pressure within certain crystals releases electricity, led to the invention of clocks with quartz timers. Their only flaw is that their vibration frequency changes over time, and in the case of public and institutional clocks it must be tested and readjusted. This can be done with an atomic clock, whose frequency is determined by molecular vibrations and never falters.

Nowadays, a high-precision pendulum clock is accurate to within three seconds a year. The accuracy of a quartz clock is a hundred to a thousand times greater than that, and the error of an atomic clock is less than one second in 100,000 years.

Everywhere in the world, timekeepers of near-perfect accuracy are available to anyone sailing a ship and are all a navigator needs to keep track of his longitude. Harrison would have had no trouble recognizing them at a glance, for no matter how different the innards, on the outside they are clearly first cousins to his silver watch. However, GPS, the Global Positioning System that is the ultimate longitude tool, would be a stranger to him.

Designed by the U.S. Air Force in the 1970s to guide troops and missiles, it consists of twenty-four satellites, eleven thousand miles out in space. They give off pulsed radio signals that can be received by portable computers on land or sea. By picking up the signals from four or more satellites, the computer is able to determine its own latitude and longitude.

When used by the military, as it was during the Persian Gulf War, GPS performs so accurately that a tank crew on the ground can fix their position within a few feet. In recent years the system has been adapted for civilians, and the newer versions are less accurate but more than sufficient for the needs of hikers, navigators, and long-distance truckers.

So longitude has lost its mystery, and watches have become so cheap that it hardly pays to have them repaired. Yet John Harrison is not forgotten. A handful of specialists came together in 1981 and called themselves the Harrison Research Group; they hold annual meetings at the Old Royal Observatory in Greenwich, to pool a year's worth of study about Harrison timekeepers. One member is building exact copies of the early wooden precision clocks. Another has been commissioned to create a modern version, combining Harrison's technology with modern materials.

All three of his sea clocks are very much alive today, thanks to Rupert Gould, the author of *The Marine Chronometer*. In 1920, as a young lieutenant commander in the Royal Navy, he had found them so "dirty, defective and corroded" that he offered to restore them, unpaid. It took twelve years of solitary labor to bring them back to gleaming good health; they are now on permanent exhibit in Greenwich, where they keep reasonably good time.

The silver watch, also restored by Gould, and on permanent display at Greenwich, is not allowed to keep time. If it did, it would have to be taken apart for cleaning, and cleaning might eventually destroy it, so it sits in silence within its showcase next to the replica made by Larcum Kendall. All the Harrison timekeepers are cared for like sacred relics; they are marveled at by tourists, by busloads of schoolchildren, and by hobbyists who know every detail of their histories.

In 1993, five hundred admirers from all over the world gathered at Harvard University to mark the three hundredth anniversary of John Harrison's birth. Papers were read, old timepieces from Harvard's Fogg Museum were inspected, escapements and balances and pendulums were discussed, but the talk always came around to Harrison, his eccentric and single-minded character, his courage, his devotion to a seemingly hopeless task. Just as his clocks are honored and cherished, so is the memory of the man called "Longitude."

GLOSSARY

Admiralty The Board of Admiralty was the British government department that managed naval affairs until 1964. Since then, it has been part of a unified Ministry of Defence.

altitude The angular height of the sun or other heavenly body; the angle made by the horizon and the line of sight to the object. When the sun is directly overhead, its altitude is 90 degrees.

angular height *See* ALTITUDE.

astrolabe An early navigation instrument that found latitude by observing the altitude of a heavenly body.

Astronomer Royal In 1675, when King Charles II founded the Royal Observatory at Greenwich, he put John Flamsteed in charge of it, as the first Astronomer Royal. The goal of the observatory was to develop a reliable lunar-distance method for finding longitude at sea. Edmond Halley became the second Astronomer Royal. James Bradley was the third, followed by Nathaniel Bliss. Nevil Maskelyne succeeded Bliss. The Astronomer Royal served as an ex officio member of the Board of Longitude.

backstaff Altitude-measuring instrument. A development of the cross-staff, the backstaff was invented in 1595 by Captain John Davis, an experienced navigator, and was also known as Davis's quadrant. It was more accurate than the cross-staff, and had the further advantage of allowing the mariner to observe the altitude of the sun without facing its blinding light.

Board of Longitude In 1714 an act of Parliament offered a reward for any method that could determine longitude at sea within certain degrees of accuracy. A Board of Longitude, consisting of twenty-two members, or commissioners, was authorized to examine and judge all proposals submitted to it, and to recommend the award of a prize if any invention met the standards of the act. The Board was composed of naval officers, politicians, and scholars.

compass An instrument used to tell direction by means of a magnetic needle turning freely on a pivot, and pointing to the magnetic north. (A pivot is a supporting point or edge that allows an object to turn with very little friction.)

cross-staff An altitude-measuring instrument; first described in two poems, written in Hebrew, by Levi ben Gershon, a fourteenth-century Provençal Jew. He called the instrument the "Revealer of Profundities."

Although far more accurate than the astrolabe, it required the navigator to sight directly into the sun, a practice that was severely damaging to the eye.

dead reckoning The earliest way of finding the position of a ship at sea. Even with the naked eye it was possible to gauge latitude—the north–south position—by estimating the angular height of the sun at noon, or of the North Star at night.

For longitude, the east–west position, dead reckoning was a matter of informed guesswork. By throwing overboard a barrel or log attached to the ship by a rope—and observing how much time (according to the hourglass) the ship took to pass the barrel—a navigator would estimate his speed. He used the compass to determine direction, and consulted his logbook to see how much time had passed since his last known position. Now that he had a rough idea of how fast he'd been sailing, in what direction, and for how long, he would make allowance for wind and current, and then attempt to calculate his longitude.

elevation *See* ALTITUDE.

escapement The timekeeping mechanism of all mechanical clocks. In a pendulum clock, the top of the pendulum's rod is attached to a bar with a hook at each end; the bar is called a pallet fork, and the hooks are called pallets. Below the pallet fork is a wheel called an escape wheel, with specially shaped teeth. The pallet fork, the escape wheel, and the pendulum together are the escapement.

The escape wheel turns with all the other wheels of the clock. As it turns, its teeth are stopped by the pallets on the pallet fork, first one pallet and then the other. The pallet fork tips one way and then the other, the pendulum swings back and forth, and the escape wheel moves forward one tooth at a time.

gimbals An arrangement for supporting an object and keeping it level while giving it freedom to rotate.

hairspring A tiny spring attached to the balance wheel of a spring-driven time-keeper. When the wheel turns, the hairspring is tightened; as the hairspring unwinds, it pushes the wheel back again, so that the balance wheel turns one way and then the other, just as a pendulum in a weight clock swings back and forth.

hourglass A device used to measure time by the flow of sand through a narrow constriction. Unlike the sundial, another early timekeeper, the hourglass was portable and could be used on cloudy days, or by candlelight.

latitude A series of imaginary lines running around the earth, parallel to the equator. These lines of latitude are used to measure distance north or south of the equator. Any place on the equator is said to have a latitude of zero degrees; the North Pole has a latitude of 90 degrees north, while the South Pole has a latitude of 90 degrees south. Degrees of latitude are divided into 60 minutes, and each of the minutes consists of 60 seconds.

longitude Just as imaginary lines of latitude are used to measure distance north or south of the equator, imaginary lines from South Pole to North Pole are used to measure east–west distances. There is no equivalent of the equator, however, so longitude has to be measured as east or west of some agreed-upon line—such as the line from North Pole to South Pole that passes through Paris, or London. *See* MERIDIANS.

All 360 degrees of the earth's circumference pass beneath the sun once in twenty-four hours. In one hour, one twenty-fourth of 360 degrees, or 15 degrees, passes beneath the sun. Because it seems that the sun is moving instead of the earth, people say that one hour of time equals 15 degrees of longitude. Each degree of longitude is divided into 60 minutes, and each minute is divided into 60 seconds of longitude.

lunars Short for the lunar-distance method of finding longitude at sea. It required, first: an accurate instrument for measuring the elevations of two celestial bodies, and the distance between them. Second: charts listing angular distances between the moon and various celestial bodies, such as the sun, at different hours of the day as they would be seen from the home port, whatever place they had started from.

If what was seen at one o'clock in the afternoon at sea took place in the skies over London at four o'clock, then the ship's time was three hours earlier, and the ship's longitude was therefore 45 degrees west of London (since 15 degrees of longitude equals one hour of time). The lunar method was time-consuming and required considerable skill in mathematics.

meridians Mapmakers think of the earth as a globe divided into 360 equal slices, resembling the slices of an apple; they go from pole to pole, passing through the equator. The lines that separate the slices are the meridians, also called the lines of longitude. The line or meridian that passes through Greenwich, in London, is used by most nations today as the prime meridian, and distance east or west of it gives the longitude.

Although one degree of longitude equals four minutes' difference in time anywhere on the globe, geographical distance is another matter. At the equator, the distance from one meridian to the next is 68 miles. As you travel north or south, the meridians come closer together until they converge at the North or South Pole, when the distance between them disappears. Navigators use a simple geometric formula to relate the distance between meridians to the number of degrees north or south of the equator.

pendulum A weighted rod suspended from a pivot that allows it to swing freely back and forth. The regularity of the swings serves to ration out the energy of the escapement as it drives the gears of the clock.

quadrant An angle-measuring instrument used at sea for observing the altitude of a heavenly body. The invention in about 1730 of a reflecting quadrant, using paired mirrors and a built-in horizon, was an important contribution to the lunar-distance system. The sextant, a later development of the quadrant, remained in use as a primary navigation tool for ships and aircraft until the middle of the twentieth century.

rate The loss or gain of a timekeeper in every twenty-four hours is called its rate. When the loss or gain is by the same amount each day, it is said to have a steady rate, and the correct time can always be calculated. A fluctuating rate makes the timekeeper unreliable.

Royal Society Royal Society of London for Improving Natural Knowledge, meaning scientific knowledge. Founded in 1660, it was originally an informal group that met periodically to discuss scientific subjects; in time it became a semiofficial adviser to the government on scientific affairs. The Society's Copley medal is the most important scientific award in Great Britain.

sailing the parallel Using the imaginary lines of latitude—the parallels—to reach a destination when there was no way of knowing longitude. The navigator would sail well to seaward of a goal whose latitude he knew, then use observation of the sun to guide the ship to that latitude, or parallel. Once within the parallel, he would sail due west or east until land was sighted.

trade winds Steady winds that blow almost constantly from the northeast toward the equator in the Northern Hemisphere, and from the southeast in the Southern Hemisphere. They provide a dependable trading route for sailing ships.

transit of Venus When the planet Venus is in a direct line between the earth and the sun, it can be seen as a small black disc crossing the sun's face. The different times taken for this crossing, or transit, as they are measured by observers in different parts of the globe, can be used to calculate the distance from Earth to Venus, and from Earth to sun. The transit takes place twice in about a century, the two times being eight years apart.

TIME LINE

Sixth century B.C.	Pythagoras teaches that earth is round
Third century B.C.	Eratosthenes calculates size of earth
Second century A.D.	Ptolemy uses meridians of longitude on maps in his *Geography*
1610	Galileo discovers Jupiter's moons, with which longitude on land can be calculated
Mid-1600s	Pendulum clock invented, introducing first reliable timekeeper

1666   Founding of French Academy of Sciences, which begins modern mapmaking

1675   Founding of England's Royal Observatory, Greenwich

1693   John Harrison born

1707   Sir Clowdisley Shovell's fleet runs aground off Scilly Isles

1713   Harrison completes his first pendulum clock

1714   British Parliament establishes Board of Longitude, offers prize for practical method of determining longitude at sea

1722   Harrison completes Brocklesby Park clock

1730   Harrison goes to London, meets Halley and Graham

c. 1730   Invention of reflecting quadrant by Hadley and Godfrey (independently)

1736   Harrison's H-1 clock tested unofficially at sea aboard HMS *Centurion*

1737   Harrison obtains grant from Board of Longitude

1739   Harrison's H-2 clock completed; never tested at sea

1740–44   HMS *Centurion* sails around world

1749   Royal Society's Copley Gold Medal awarded to Harrison

1755   Tobias Mayer sends lunar tables to Lord Anson

1757–59   Captain Campbell tests Mayer's lunar tables, under wartime restrictions

1760   Harrison's H-3 clock completed; never tested at sea.
        Harrison shows H-4 silver watch to Board of Longitude

1761   Nevil Maskelyne tests Mayer's lunar tables on voyage to
        St. Helena

1761–62 Sea trial to Jamaica for H-4; Board of Longitude will not
          accept results

1763   Publication of Maskelyne's *British Mariner's Guide*,
        followed (1767) by *The Nautical Almanac*

1763   Maskelyne sails to Barbados to test Mayer's recently
        improved lunar tables and to check sea trial of H-4

1764   William Harrison sails for Barbados for sea trial of H-4

1764   John Harrison invited to join Royal Society, but declines
        honor

1765   Maskelyne appointed Astronomer Royal

1765   New act of Parliament changes rules for longitude prize

1765   Harrison awarded one-half the prize money, on condition
        he disclose mechanism of H-4

1767   Unfavorable results of H-4's trial at Greenwich published

1772   Captain James Cook sails on his second Pacific voyage,
        taking Harrison-Kendall watch and others for testing as
        longitude devices

1772   George III completes successful testing of H-5 watch at
        Richmond

1773   After parliamentary debate, an act authorizes payment to
        Harrison equal to second half of longitude prize

1775   Cook returns with enthusiastic reports on Harrison-
        Kendall watch

1776   John Harrison dies

BIBLIOGRAPHY

Andrewes, William. *The Quest for Longitude*. Cambridge, Mass.: Collection of Historical Scientific Instruments, Harvard University, 1996.

Anson, George. *A Voyage Round the World*. London: Oxford University Press, 1974.

Ayling, Stanley. *George the Third*. New York: Knopf, 1972.

Beaglehole, J. C. *The Life of Captain James Cook*. Stanford, Calif.: Stanford University Press, 1974.

Blumberg, Rhoda. *The Remarkable Voyages of Captain Cook*. New York: Bradbury Press, 1991.

Brooke, John. *King George III*. London: Constable, 1972.

Brown, Lloyd A. *The Story of Maps*. Boston: Little, Brown, 1949.

Gould, Rupert T. *The Marine Chronometer*. London: J. D. Potter, 1923.

Hart, Roger. *English Life in the Eighteenth Century*. New York: G. P. Putnam's Sons, 1970.

Heaps, Leo. *Log of the Centurion*. New York: Macmillan, 1973.

Howse, Derek. *Greenwich Time*. Oxford: Oxford University Press, 1980.

————. *Nevil Maskelyne, The Seaman's Astronomer*. Cambridge: Cambridge University Press, 1989.

Landes, David S. *Revolution in Time*. Cambridge, Mass.: Harvard University Press, 1983.

Laycock, William. *The Lost Science of John "Longitude" Harrison*. Kent, England: Brant Wright, 1976.

Massingham, Hugh and Pauline. *The London Anthology*. London: Spring Books, n.d.

Plumb, J. H. *England in the Eighteenth Century*. Baltimore: Penguin Books, 1963.

Quill, Humphrey. *John Harrison, the Man Who Found Longitude*. London: Baker, 1966.

Sobel, Dava. *Longitude*. New York: Walker, 1995.

Thomas, R. *Interesting and Authentic Narratives of the Most Remarkable Shipwrecks*. Freeport, N.Y.: Books for Libraries Press, 1970. (Reprint; first published 1835.)

Wilcox, L. A. *Anson's Voyage*. New York: St. Martin's Press, 1970.

INDEX